JUMP Math
Book 3 Part 2 of 2

Contents

Unit 10: Number Sense: Division   1

Unit 11: Patterns and Algebra: Patterns and Equations   31

Unit 12: Number Sense: Fractions   50

Unit 13: Measurement: Time   70

Unit 14: Measurement: Capacity, Mass, and Temperature   91

Unit 15: Number Sense: Estimating   108

Unit 16: Number Sense: Money   119

Unit 17: Geometry: Transformations and 3-D Shapes   157

Unit 18: Probability and Data Management: Graphs and Probability   182

jump math™

MULTIPLYING POTENTIAL.

JUMP Math
One Yonge Street, Suite 1014
Toronto, Ontario M5E 1E5
Canada
www.jumpmath.org

Writers: Dr. Anna Klebanov, Saverio Mercurio, Dr. Sohrab Rahbar
Editors: Megan Burns, Liane Tsui, Julie Takasaki, Natalie Francis, Jackie Dulson, Janice Dyer, Dawn Hunter, Jodi Rauch, Strong Finish Editorial Design
Layout and Illustrations: Linh Lam, Fely Guinasao-Fernandes, Sawyer Paul
Cover Design: Blakeley Words+Pictures
Cover Photograph: © Shutterstock/irin-k

ISBN 978-1-927457-96-2

Third printing May 2018

Printed and bound in Canada

Welcome to JUMP Math

Entering the world of JUMP Math means believing that every child has the capacity to be fully numerate and to love math. Founder and mathematician John Mighton has used this premise to develop his innovative teaching method. The resulting resources isolate and describe concepts so clearly and incrementally that everyone can understand them.

JUMP Math is comprised of teacher's guides (which are the heart of our program), interactive whiteboard lessons, student assessment & practice books, evaluation materials, outreach programs, and teacher training. All of this is presented on the JUMP Math website: **www.jumpmath.org**.

Teacher's guides are available on the website for free use. Read the introduction to the teacher's guides before you begin using these resources. This will ensure that you understand both the philosophy and the methodology of JUMP Math. The assessment & practice books are designed for use by students, with adult guidance. Each student will have unique needs and it is important to provide the student with the appropriate support and encouragement as he or she works through the material.

Allow students to discover the concepts by themselves as much as possible. Mathematical discoveries can be made in small, incremental steps. The discovery of a new step is like untangling the parts of a puzzle. It is exciting and rewarding.

Students will need to answer the questions marked with a ▯ in a notebook. Grid paper notebooks should always be on hand for answering extra questions or when additional room for calculation is needed.

Contents

PART 1
Unit 1: Patterns and Algebra: Patterns

PA3-1	Counting On	1
PA3-2	Number Patterns Made by Adding	2
PA3-3	Counting Backwards	4
PA3-4	Number Patterns Made by Subtracting	6
PA3-5	Number Patterns Made by Adding or Subtracting	8
PA3-6	Number Patterns and Rules	10
PA3-7	Ordinal Numbers	13
PA3-8	Number Patterns in Tables	15
PA3-9	T-tables	17
PA3-10	Attributes	20
PA3-11	Repeating Patterns	22
PA3-12	Exploring Patterns	25

Unit 2: Number Sense: Place Value

NS3-1	Place Value—Ones, Tens, and Hundreds	28
NS3-2	Base Ten Blocks	30
NS3-3	Expanded Form	33
NS3-4	Writing and Reading Number Words	35
NS3-5	Writing and Reading 3-Digit Numbers	38
NS3-6	Showing Numbers in Different Ways	39
NS3-7	Comparing Numbers with Base Ten Models	42
NS3-8	Comparing Numbers by Place Value	44
NS3-9	Placing Numbers in Order	47
NS3-10	Differences of 10 and of 100	49
NS3-11	Regrouping of Ones, Tens, and Hundreds	52
NS3-12	Addition with Regrouping—Tens	55
NS3-13	Addition with Regrouping—Hundreds	58
NS3-14	Subtraction without Regrouping	61
NS3-15	Subtraction with Regrouping—Tens	63
NS3-16	Subtraction with Regrouping—Hundreds	66
NS3-17	Problems and Puzzles	70

Unit 3: Number Sense: Mental Addition and Subtraction

NS3-18	Introduction to Mental Math	72
NS3-19	Making 10 to Add	76
NS3-20	Doubles	79
NS3-21	Adding Tens and Adding Ones	81
NS3-22	Subtraction Fluency	83
NS3-23	Subtracting Mentally	85

NS3-24	Parts and Totals	87
NS3-25	More Parts and Totals	90
NS3-26	Sums and Differences	93

Unit 4: Measurement: Length and Perimeter

ME3-1	Measuring in Centimetres	95
ME3-2	Measuring and Drawing in Centimetres	98
ME3-3	Metres	100
ME3-4	Metres and Centimetres	102
ME3-5	Kilometres	104
ME3-6	Choosing Units	106
ME3-7	Measuring Around a Shape—Perimeter	109
ME3-8	Exploring Perimeter	112

Unit 5: Geometry: Shapes

G3-1	Introduction to Classifying Data	114
G3-2	Venn Diagrams	116
G3-3	Sides and Vertices of Shapes	120
G3-4	Sorting Polygons	123
G3-5	Introduction to Angles	125
G3-6	Shapes with Equal Sides	129
G3-7	Quadrilaterals	132
G3-8	More Quadrilaterals	135
G3-9	Parallel Sides	138
G3-10	Special Quadrilaterals	141
G3-11	Comparing Special Quadrilaterals	143
G3-12	Polygons (Advanced)	145
G3-13	Congruent Shapes	147
G3-14	Symmetry	150

Unit 6: Number Sense: Skip Counting and Multiplication

NS3-27	Even and Odd Numbers	153
NS3-28	Repeated Addition	155
NS3-29	Skip Counting by 2s and 4s	157
NS3-30	Skip Counting by 5s and 10s	159
NS3-31	Skip Counting by 3s	160
NS3-32	Multiplication and Repeated Addition	162
NS3-33	Multiplication and Equal Groups	164
NS3-34	Multiplying by Skip Counting	167
NS3-35	Arrays	169
NS3-36	Patterns in Multiplication of Even Numbers	172
NS3-37	Patterns in Multiplication of Odd Numbers	174
NS3-38	Concepts in Multiplication (1)	176

Unit 7: Number Sense: Multiplication

NS3-39	Using Doubles to Multiply	178
NS3-40	Brackets	180
NS3-41	Multiplying by Adding On	181
NS3-42	Finding Easier Ways to Multiply	183
NS3-43	Multiplying by 1 and 0	185
NS3-44	Multiplication Charts (1)	187
NS3-45	Multiplication Charts (2)	189
NS3-46	The Associative Property	191
NS3-47	Concepts in Multiplication (2)	193

Unit 8: Measurement: Area

ME3-9	Shapes and Area	195
ME3-10	Measuring Area with Different Units	198
ME3-11	Skip Counting to Find Area	200
ME3-12	Multiplying to Find Area	202
ME3-13	Estimating and Measuring Area	204

Unit 9: Probability and Data Management: Charts

PDM3-1	Tally Charts	207
PDM3-2	Line Plots	209
PDM3-3	Reading Line Plots	212

PART 2
Unit 10: Number Sense: Division

NS3-48	Sharing When You Know the Number of Sets	1
NS3-49	Sharing When You Know the Number in Each Set	3
NS3-50	Sets	5
NS3-51	Two Ways of Sharing	7
NS3-52	Two Ways of Sharing: Word Problems	9
NS3-53	Division and Addition	11
NS3-54	Dividing by Skip Counting	13
NS3-55	The Two Meanings of Division	15
NS3-56	Division and Multiplication	17
NS3-57	Knowing When to Multiply or Divide	19
NS3-58	Knowing When to Multiply or Divide: Word Problems	21
NS3-59	Multiplication and Division (Review)	23
NS3-60	Rows and Columns	25
NS3-61	Multiplication and Division Word Problems	28

Unit 11: Patterns and Algebra: Patterns and Equations

| PA3-13 | Geometric Patterns | 31 |

PA3-14	Patterns on Number Lines	34
PA3-15	Patterns in Charts	37
PA3-16	Equal and Not Equal	40
PA3-17	Addition Equations	42
PA3-18	Subtraction Equations	45
PA3-19	Using Letters for Unknown Numbers	48

Unit 12: Number Sense: Fractions

NS3-62	Equal Paper Folding	50
NS3-63	Unit Fractions	52
NS3-64	Writing Fractions	54
NS3-65	Fractions and Pattern Blocks	57
NS3-66	Equal Parts of Shapes	59
NS3-67	Different Shapes, Same Fractions	61
NS3-68	Fractions of a Set	63
NS3-69	Comparing Fractions	65
NS3-70	Fraction Squares	68

Unit 13: Measurement: Time

ME3-14	Digital Clocks	70
ME3-15	Analog Clock Faces and Hands	71
ME3-16	The Minute Hand	74
ME3-17	Time to the Five Minutes	77
ME3-18	Half and Quarter Hours	79
ME3-19	Minutes to the Hour	82
ME3-20	Timelines	85
ME3-21	Intervals of Time	87
ME3-22	Units of Time	89

Unit 14: Measurement: Capacity, Mass, and Temperature

ME3-23	Capacity	91
ME3-24	Fractions of a Litre	94
ME3-25	Mass	97
ME3-26	Grams and Kilograms	99
ME3-27	Mass Word Problems	102
ME3-28	Fractions of a Kilogram	104
ME3-29	Temperature	106

Unit 15: Number Sense: Estimating

NS3-71	Rounding Tens	108
NS3-72	Estimating	110
NS3-73	Estimating Quantities	112
NS3-74	Place Value: Ones, Tens, Hundreds, and Thousands	115
NS3-75	Adding to Make a 4-Digit Number	117

Unit 16: Number Sense: Money

NS3-76	Counting by 5s and 25s	119
NS3-77	Counting Coins	121
NS3-78	Counting On by Two or More Coin Values	124
NS3-79	What Coins Are Missing?	127
NS3-80	Least Number of Coins	130
NS3-81	Finding the Difference Using Mental Math	133
NS3-82	Counting Money with Dollars	136
NS3-83	Representing Money to 10 Dollars	139
NS3-84	Dollars and Cents Notation	142
NS3-85	Counting Money to 100 Dollars	144
NS3-86	Multiplication and Money	147
NS3-87	Making Payments and Earning Money	150
NS3-88	Rounding to the Nearest 5 (Advanced)	152
NS3-89	Giving Change (Advanced)	154

Unit 17: Geometry: Transformation and 3-D Shapes

G3-15	Translations	157
G3-16	Translations on Maps	160
G3-17	Reflections	163
G3-18	Flips, Slides, and Turns	165
G3-19	3-D Shapes	169
G3-20	Building Pyramids and Prisms	172
G3-21	Faces of 3-D Shapes	175
G3-22	Matching 3-D Shapes	178
G3-23	Shapes with Curved Surfaces	180

Unit 18: Probability and Data Management: Graphs and Probability

PDM3-4	Introduction to Pictographs	182
PDM3-5	Pictographs	185
PDM3-6	Creating Pictographs	187
PDM3-7	Introduction to Bar Graphs	189
PDM3-8	Bar Graphs	192
PDM3-9	Scales on Bar Graphs	195
PDM3-10	Comparing Graphs	199
PDM3-11	Surveys	201
PDM3-12	Outcomes	204
PDM3-13	Even Chance	206
PDM3-14	Even, Likely, and Unlikely	209
PDM3-15	Fair Games	211
PDM3-16	Expectation	214

NS3-48 Sharing When You Know the Number of Sets

Four friends want to share 12 cookies. They set out 4 plates.

They put I cookie on
each plate, then repeat.

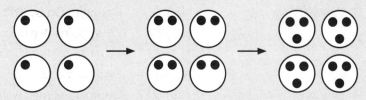

Each plate holds a **set** (or group) of 3 cookies.

When 12 cookies are **divided** (or shared equally) into 4 sets, there are 3 cookies **in each set**.

1. Put an equal number of cookies on each plate.
   Hint: Draw the plates, then place I cookie at a time.

   a) 6 cookies   3 plates

   b) 9 cookies   3 plates

   c) 8 cookies   2 plates

   d) 5 plates   10 cookies

   e) 2 plates   6 cookies

   f) 4 plates   12 cookies

   g) 4 plates   8 cookies

   h) 2 plates   12 cookies

2. Draw dots for the things being shared equally. Draw circles for the sets.

a) 3 wagons

9 students

How many students in each wagon?

b) 15 stamps

3 pages

How many stamps on each page?

_____ students in each wagon

_____ stamps on each page

c) 4 boats

12 students

How many students on each boat?

d) 2 boxes

10 pens

How many pens in each box?

_____ students on each boat

_____ pens in each box

3. Draw a picture or make a model to solve the problem.

a) 4 friends share 8 tickets.
How many tickets does each friend get?

b) 12 chairs are placed in 3 rows.
How many chairs are in each row?

c) 24 flowers are planted in 6 rows.
How many flowers are in each row?

d) Edmond earned 20 dollars for his work. He worked 5 hours.
How much did he earn each hour?
Hint: Draw dots for dollars and circles for hours.

e) Kate earned 15 dollars for her work. She worked 3 hours.
How much did she earn each hour?

Ivan has 20 apples. He wants to put 5 apples in each bag.

To find out how many bags he needs, he starts by counting out 5 apples.

He then keeps counting out sets of 5 apples until he has used all 20 apples.

He can make 4 bags. When 20 apples are divided into sets of 5 apples, there are 4 sets.

1. Put the correct number of dots in each set.

a) ⬭⬭⬭⬭ ●
   2 dots in each set

b) ● ● ● ● ● ●
   3 dots in each set

c) ● ● ● ● ● ● ● ●
   2 dots in each set

d) ● ● ● ● ● ● ● ● ●
   3 dots in each set

e) ● ● ● ● ● ● ● ● ● ●
   5 dots in each set

f) ● ● ● ● ● ● ● ● ● ● ● ●
   3 dots in each set

2. Divide the array into the given number of sets.

a) sets of 2

● ● ●
● ● ●

b) sets of 3

● ● ●
● ● ●

c) sets of 3

● ● ● ●
● ● ● ●
● ● ● ●

d) sets of 4

● ● ● ●
● ● ● ●
● ● ● ●

3. Draw a picture to solve the problem. Hint: Start by drawing a circle and placing the correct number of dots in the circle.

a) 12 dots

   4 dots in each set

   How many sets? _____

b) 15 dots

   5 dots in each set

   How many sets? _____

4. Draw dots for the things being divided equally.
Draw circles for the sets.

a) 10 students

   5 students in each wagon

   How many wagons?

      _____ wagons

b) 12 stamps

   4 stamps on each page

   How many pages?

      _____ pages

c) 20 books

   4 books on each shelf

   How many shelves?

      _____ shelves

d) 15 fish

   5 fish in each tank

   How many tanks?

      _____ tanks

5. Sam has 10 oranges. He wants to sell bags of 2 oranges. How many bags can he sell?

6. Emma has 12 books. She wants to put 3 books in each bag. How many bags does she need?

7. Raj has 15 stamps. He wants to put 5 stamps on each page of his stamp book. How many pages will he need?

8. A sailboat can hold 3 students. There are 12 students. How many sailboats are needed?

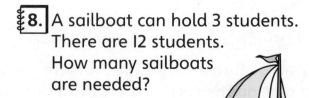

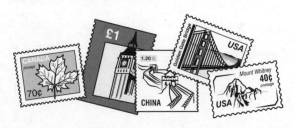

NS3-50 Sets

12 students go canoeing.
There are 4 canoes.
A canoe holds 3 students.

What has been shared or divided into sets?   *Students.*

How many sets are there?   *There are 4 sets of students.*

How many are in each set?   *There are 3 students in each set.*

1. Fill in the blanks.

   a)

   What has been shared or divided

   into sets? _____

   How many sets? _____

   How many in each set? _____

   b)

   What has been shared or divided

   into sets? _____

   How many sets? _____

   How many in each set? _____

2. Draw a picture to show the situation. Use circles for sets and dots for items.

   a) 3 sets   4 items in each set

   b) 4 sets   5 items in each set

   c) 2 groups   3 items in each group

   d) 2 groups   4 items in each group

3. Fill in the table.

		What Has Been Shared or Divided into Sets?	How Many Sets?	How Many in Each Set?
a)	15 students 3 students in each boat 5 boats	students	5	3
b)	5 friends 20 cookies 4 cookies for each friend			
c)	18 oranges 6 boxes 3 oranges in each box			
d)	4 dogs 20 spots 5 spots on each dog			
e)	5 stamps on each page 35 stamps 7 pages			
f)	3 playgrounds 12 swings 4 swings in each playground			
g)	5 people in each house 10 people 2 houses			
h)	20 chairs 5 rows 4 chairs in each row			

Iva has 12 cookies. There are two ways she can share or divide her cookies equally.

Method 1:
She can decide how many sets.

Example: She wants to make 3 sets. She draws 3 circles.

She puts one cookie in each circle.

She continues until she uses all 12 cookies.

There are 4 cookies in each set.

Method 2:
She can decide how many in each set.

Example: She puts 3 cookies in each set.

She counts out sets of 3 until she uses all 12 cookies.

3   6   9   12

She makes 4 sets.

1. Share 12 dots equally. How many dots are in each set?
   Place one dot at a time.

   a) 3 sets

   There are _____ dots in each set.

   b) 4 sets

   There are _____ dots in each set.

2. Share 15 dots equally. How many dots are in each set?

   a) 3 sets

   There are _____ dots in each set.

   b) 5 sets

   There are _____ dots in each set.

3. Share the triangles equally among the sets.
Hint: Count the triangles first.

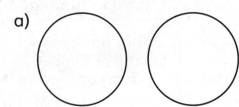

a)

b)

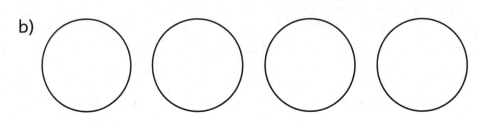

4. Share the squares equally among the sets.

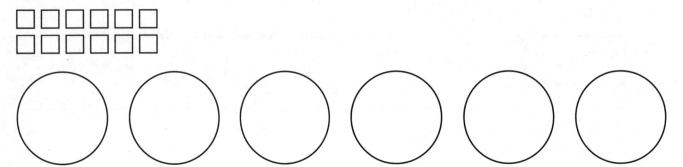

5. Draw a picture to group 12 dots equally.

a) 3 dots in each set

b) 6 dots in each set

6. Show two ways you could put 10 apples in baskets.

a) Put 5 apples in each basket.

b) Put 2 apples in each basket.

I. Fill in what you know. Write a question mark for what you don't know.

		What Has Been Shared or Divided into Sets?	How Many Sets?	How Many in Each Set?
a)	Jay has 15 stamps. He puts 5 stamps on each page of his book.	*stamps*	*?*	*5*
b)	20 campers go canoeing in 10 canoes.	*campers*	*10*	*?*
c)	Don has 15 pens. He puts them into 3 boxes.			
d)	4 friends share 20 apples.			
e)	Grace has 10 cookies. She puts 5 on each plate.			
f)	12 campers go sailing. There are 4 campers in each boat.			
g)	12 fruit bars are shared among 3 campers.			
h)	8 chairs are in 2 rows.			
i)	There are 10 friends. 2 friends fit in a go-cart.			
j)	There are 20 books on a bookshelf. Each shelf holds 5 books.			

2. Draw dots to show the answer.

a) 10 dots   5 sets

_____ dots in each set

b) 6 dots   3 dots in each set

_____ sets

c) 15 dots   5 dots in each set

_____ sets

d) 8 dots   4 sets

_____ dots in each set

e) 6 chairs in 2 rows

How many chairs are in

each row? _____

f) Ron has 8 pencils.
He puts 2 pencils in each box.

How many boxes does

he use? _____

g) 4 boys share 12 marbles.

How many marbles does each

boy get? _____

h) Sandy has 9 pears.
She gives 3 pears to each friend.

How many friends receive

pears? _____

i) 15 children go sailing in 3 boats.

How many children are in

each boat? _____

j) Lewis has 16 stickers.
He puts 4 on a page.

How many pages does

he use? _____

NS3-53 Division and Addition

The picture shows 12 objects divided into sets of 4. There are **3** sets.

The **division sentence** is 12 ÷ 4 = 3.

1. Write a division sentence for the picture.

a)

b)

c)

d)

2. The answer to the division sentence shows the number of sets.
   Draw a picture for the division sentence.

a) 15 ÷ 5 = 3

b) 12 ÷ 2 = 6

c) 20 ÷ 4 = 5

d) 16 ÷ 8 = 2

e) 24 ÷ 6 = 4

You can rewrite any division sentence as an addition sentence.

Example: 12 ÷ 3 = 4 because 12 divided into sets of size 3 equals 4 sets.

So   3   +   3   +   3   +   3   =   12.

Adding four 3s equals 12.

3. Draw a picture and write an **addition** sentence for the **division** sentence.

a) 6 ÷ 2 = 3

$\underline{\quad 2 + 2 + 2 = 6 \qquad\qquad}$

b) 8 ÷ 4 = 2

$\underline{\qquad\qquad\qquad\qquad\qquad}$

c) 15 ÷ 5 = 3

d) 9 ÷ 3 = 3

$\underline{\qquad\qquad\qquad\qquad\qquad}$ $\underline{\qquad\qquad\qquad\qquad\qquad}$

4. Draw a picture and write a **division** sentence for the **addition** sentence.

a) 4 + 4 + 4 = 12

$\underline{\quad 12 ÷ 4 = 3 \qquad\qquad}$

b) 3 + 3 + 3 + 3 + 3 = 15

$\underline{\qquad\qquad\qquad\qquad\qquad}$

c) 6 + 6 + 6 = 18

d) 2 + 2 + 2 + 2 + 2 = 10

$\underline{\qquad\qquad\qquad\qquad\qquad}$ $\underline{\qquad\qquad\qquad\qquad\qquad}$

NS3-54 Dividing by Skip Counting

You can divide by skip counting on a number line. Example: Find 12 ÷ 3.

It takes 4 skips of size 3 to get to 12.   **3 + 3 + 3 + 3 = 12 so 12 ÷ 3 = 4**

1. Use the number line to complete the division sentence.

a)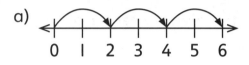

6 ÷ 2 = ___3___

b)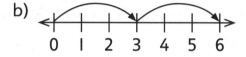

6 ÷ 3 = _____

2. Use the number line to divide.

a)

8 ÷ 4 = _____

b)

4 ÷ 4 = _____

c)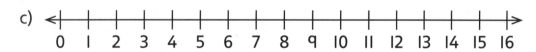

16 ÷ 4 = _____

3. What division sentence does the picture show?

a)

_____

b)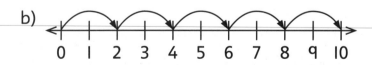

_____

c)

_____

You can also divide by skip counting on your fingers.

Example: To find **6 ÷ 2**, count by 2s until you reach 6.

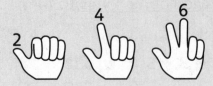

The number of fingers you have up when you stop is the answer.
So 6 ÷ 2 = 3.

4. Find the answer by skip counting on your fingers.

a) 10 ÷ 2 = _____   b) 8 ÷ 2 = _____   c) 4 ÷ 2 = _____   d) 9 ÷ 3 = _____

e) 10 ÷ 5 = _____   f) 15 ÷ 5 = _____   g) 25 ÷ 5 = _____   h) 20 ÷ 5 = _____

i) 12 ÷ 3 = _____   j) 6 ÷ 3 = _____   k) 12 ÷ 2 = _____   l) 5 ÷ 5 = _____

m) 2 ÷ 2 = _____   n) 30 ÷ 5 = _____   o) 15 ÷ 3 = _____   p) 20 ÷ 4 = _____

q) 16 ÷ 2 = _____   r) 3 ÷ 3 = _____   s) 20 ÷ 2 = _____   t) 12 ÷ 4 = _____

5. Fill in the missing numbers on the hands. Then divide by skip counting.

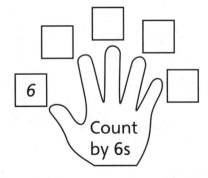
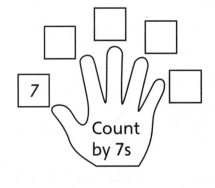

a) 18 ÷ 6 = _____   b) 24 ÷ 6 = _____   c) 12 ÷ 6 = _____

d) 21 ÷ 7 = _____   e) 35 ÷ 7 = _____   f) 28 ÷ 7 = _____

g) 30 ÷ 6 = _____   h) 6 ÷ 6 = _____   i) 7 ÷ 7 = _____

6. Find the answer by skip counting.

a) Three friends share 12 stickers.
How many stickers does each get?

b) Twenty-four students sit at 6 tables.
How many students are at each table?

David buys 12 fish from a pet store. He has 4 fish bowls.

How many fish can David put in each bowl? David counts by 4s to find out:

 "I could put one fish in each bowl."
(4 are placed)

 "I could put one more in each bowl."
(8 are placed)

 "I could put one more in each bowl."
(12 are placed)

He raised 3 fingers, so he knows that **12 ÷ 4 = 3**. He puts 3 fish in each bowl.

1. Count the lines. Then divide the lines into 2 equal groups.
   Hint: Skip count by 2s to decide how many to put in each group.

   a) (| | |)(| | |)

   _____ lines altogether

   _____ in each group

   b) | | | | | | | | | |

   _____ lines altogether

   _____ in each group

   c) | | | | | | | | | | | |

   _____ lines altogether

   _____ in each group

   d) | | | | | | | |

   _____ lines altogether

   _____ in each group

2. Count the objects. Then divide the objects into equal groups.
   Hint: Skip count by the number of groups to decide how many to put in each group.

   a) 3 equal groups

   b) 5 equal groups

   c) 2 equal groups

   d) 4 equal groups

   ■ ■ ■ ■ ■ ■ ■ ■ ■ ■ ■ ■

Here are two ways to describe the picture below.

When 15 things are divided into 5 sets, there are 3 things in each set: 15 ÷ 5 = 3.

When 15 things are divided into sets of size 3, there are 5 sets: 15 ÷ 3 = 5.

3. Fill in the blanks. Then write two division sentences.

a)

_____ lines   _____ sets

_____ lines in each set

_____ ÷ _____ = _____

_____ ÷ _____ = _____

b)

_____ lines   _____ sets

_____ lines in each set

_____ ÷ _____ = _____

_____ ÷ _____ = _____

c)

_____ lines   _____ sets

_____ lines in each set

_____ ÷ _____ = _____

_____ ÷ _____ = _____

4. Fill in the blanks. Then write two division sentences.

a)

_____ squares   _____ sets

_____ squares in each set

_____

_____

b)

_____ dots   _____ sets

_____ dots in each set

_____

_____

c)

_____ stars   _____ sets

_____ stars in each set

_____

_____

5. Solve the problem by drawing a picture. Then write a division sentence for your answer.

a) 9 triangles, 3 sets
How many triangles in each set?

b) 12 squares, 4 squares in each set
How many sets?

c) 30 people, 5 vans
How many people in each van?

d) 20 campers, 4 in each tent
How many tents?

Remember: 10 ÷ 2 = 5 tells us that 10 ÷ 5 = 2, and 5 × 2 = 10 tells us that 2 × 5 = 10. You can rewrite any **division** sentence as a **multiplication** sentence.

Example: 10 divided into sets of size 2 equals 5 sets or **10 ÷ 2 = 5**.

You can rewrite this as: 5 sets of size 2 equals 10 or **5 × 2 = 10**.

I. Write two multiplication sentences and two division sentences for the picture.

a) | | | | | | | | | | | | | | | |

_____

_____

_____

b) | | | | | | | | | | | | | | | |

_____

_____

_____

c)

_____

_____

_____

d)

_____

_____

_____

_____

2. Fill in the blanks.

a) | || | || | || |

_____ lines in total

_____ lines in each set

_____ sets

b) | |||| | |||| | |||| | |||| |

_____ lines in total

_____ sets

_____ lines in each set

c) | |||| | |||| | |||| |

_____ lines in each group

_____ groups

_____ lines

d) | || | || | || | || | || | || |

_____ lines in each group

_____ lines

_____ groups

3. Draw a picture to show the situation.

a) 12 lines altogether, 3 lines in each set, 4 sets

b) 8 lines, 4 lines in each set, 2 sets

c) 5 sets, 3 lines in each set, 15 lines in total

d) 12 lines, 2 sets, 6 lines in each set

e) 10 lines, 5 in each set, 2 sets

4. Draw a picture to show the situation. Then write two division sentences and two multiplication sentences.

a) 20 lines, 5 sets, 4 lines in each set

b) 15 lines, 5 lines in each set, 3 sets

5. Draw a picture to find the missing information.

a) 5 lines in each set

_____ sets

15 lines altogether

b) 18 lines

_____ lines in each set

3 sets

c) _____ lines in total

3 groups

4 lines in each group

NS3-57 Knowing When to Multiply or Divide

1. Multiply or divide to find the missing information (?).

	Total Number of Things	Number of Sets	Number in Each Set	Multiplication or Division Sentence
a)	?	8	2	$8 \times 2 = 16$
b)	27	3	?	$27 \div 3 = 9$
c)	20	?	5	
d)	10	2	?	
e)	?	4	8	
f)	21	7	?	
g)	32	8	?	
h)	45	?	9	
i)	64	8	?	
j)	81	9	?	
k)	72	?	8	
l)	16	4	?	
m)	28	?	7	
n)	42	6	?	
o)	?	8	9	

2. Write a multiplication or division sentence to solve the problem.

a) 15 things in total

5 things in each set

_____

How many sets?

_____

b) 5 sets

4 things in each set

_____

How many in total?

_____

c) 24 things in total

6 sets

_____

How many in each set?

_____

d) 4 groups

7 things in each group

_____

How many in total?

_____

e) 2 things in each set

12 things in total

_____

How many sets?

_____

f) 5 groups

45 things in total

_____

How many in

each group? _____

g) 5 things in each set

4 sets

_____

How many in total?

_____

h) 8 things in each set

3 sets

_____

How many in total?

_____

i) 16 things in total

8 sets

_____

How many in each set?

_____

j) 3 things in each set

6 sets

_____

How many in total?

_____

k) 12 things in total

4 sets

_____

How many in each set?

_____

l) 20 things in total

4 sets

_____

How many in each set?

_____

3. Make up your own problem with things in sets.
Draw a picture to solve it.

1. Fill in the table. Use a question mark to show what you don't know.

		Total Number of Things	Number of Sets	Number in Each Set	Multiplication or Division Sentence
a)	20 people 4 vans	20	4	?	$20 \div 4 = ?$
b)	3 marbles in each jar 6 jars	?	6	3	$6 \times 3 = ?$
c)	15 flowers 5 pots				
d)	4 chairs at each table 2 tables				
e)	20 flowers 4 in each row				
f)	6 seats in each row 2 rows				
g)	18 houses 9 houses on each block				
h)	15 chairs 3 rows				
i)	6 tents 3 campers in each tent				
j)	9 boxes 3 sea shells in each box				
k)	6 legs on each insect 42 legs				

2. Find the missing number in each part of Question 1.

The fact family for the multiplication sentence **3 × 5 = 15** is:

| 3 × 5 = 15 | 5 × 3 = 15 | 15 ÷ 3 = 5 | 15 ÷ 5 = 3 |

3. Complete the fact family for the given multiplication or division sentence.

a) 4 × 2 = 8

_____

_____

_____

b) 5 × 6 = 30

_____

_____

_____

c) 10 ÷ 2 = 5

_____

_____

_____

d) 12 ÷ 4 = 3

_____

_____

_____

e) 9 × 3 = 27

_____

_____

_____

f) 6 × 8 = 48

_____

_____

_____

4. Armand plants 24 trees in 3 rows. How many trees are in each row?

5. Alex plants 4 rows of trees with 7 in each row. How many trees did she plant?

6. A canoe can hold 3 people.

a) How many canoes are needed for 21 people?

b) How many people can go canoeing with 5 canoes?

7. You need 3 tickets to ride the roller coaster at the amusement park.

a) Mandy, Tom, and Jane want to ride the roller coaster. How many tickets will they need altogether?

b) How many tickets are needed for 8 people?

BONUS ▶ Kim has 17 tickets. If she pays for herself and 4 of her friends, how many tickets will she have left?

NS3-59 Multiplication and Division (Review)

1. What is the fact family for $2 \times 3 = 6$?

2. Find the mystery number.

a) I am a multiple of 2.
I am greater than 10 and less than 13.

b) I am a multiple of 3.
I am between 13 and 20.
I am an even number.

3. A hummingbird feeds 6 times each hour.
How many times does it feed in 7 hours?

4. Apple trees in an orchard are planted in 7 rows.
There are 4 trees in each row.

a) How many trees are in the orchard?

b) How did you find your answer? Mental math?
Skip counting? A picture?

5. 6 is twice as much as (or double) 3. Is 6×5 twice as much
as 3×5? Use an array to decide.

6. Fill in the blanks. Then write two division sentences and
one multiplication sentence using the boxes.

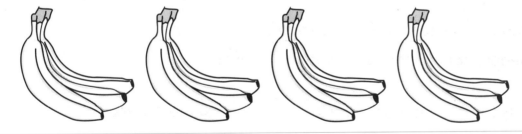

_____ bananas

_____ bananas in each bunch

_____ bunches

☐ ÷ ☐ = ☐   ☐ ÷ ☐ = ☐   ☐ × ☐ = ☐

7. A shelf is 40 cm long. How many stuffed animals of each type would fit end to end?

a)

5 cm wide

b)

4 cm wide

c)

8 cm wide

8. Picture A shows that 5 sets of 4 equals 3 sets of 4 plus 2 sets of 4.

A. |

What does picture B show?

B. |

9. Fill in the blanks with the numbers 2, 3, and 4 to make the number sentence true.

a) _____ × _____ + _____ = 11   b) _____ ÷ _____ + _____ = 5

10. Clara divided one number by another and got the answer 3. What might the numbers have been?

11. Make up a story problem for the number sentence. Draw a picture with counters to show the answer.

a) 5 × 4 = 20   b) 12 ÷ 3 = 4

BONUS ▶ A hawk's nest holds at least 3 eggs and at most 5 eggs.

a) What is the **least** number of eggs 3 nests would hold?

b) What is the **greatest** number of eggs 3 nests would hold?

NS3-60 Rows and Columns

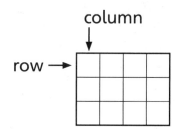

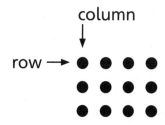

1. Number the rows and columns. Write the total number of small squares in the array.

a)

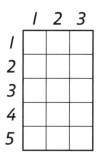

___5___ rows

___3___ columns

total ___5 × 3 = 15___

or ___3 × 5 = 15___

b)

_____ rows

_____ columns

total _____

or _____

c)
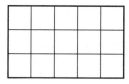

_____ rows

_____ columns

total _____

or _____

2. Count the rows and columns. Write the total number of dots in the array.

a)
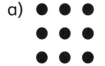

___4___ rows

___3___ columns

total ___4 × 3 = 12___

or ___3 × 4 = 12___

b)

_____ rows

_____ columns

total _____

or _____

c)

_____ rows

_____ columns

total _____

or _____

3. Write a multiplication sentence for the total number of dots. Then write another multiplication sentence and two division sentences for the array.

a)

● ● ● ● ●
● ● ● ● ●
● ● ● ● ●

___3___ rows ___5___ columns

total ___3 × 5 = 15___

___5 × 3 = 15___

___15 ÷ 5 = 3___

___15 ÷ 3 = 5___

b)

● ● ● ● ● ●
● ● ● ● ● ●

_____ rows _____ columns

total _____

_____

_____

_____

4. The table gives the number of rows and columns in arrays. Write two multiplication sentences and two division sentences for each array.

	Rows	Columns	Total	Sentences	
a)	5	2	10	5 × 2 = 10 2 × 5 = 10	10 ÷ 5 = 2 10 ÷ 2 = 5
b)	6	4	24		
c)	3	7	21		
d)	7	8	56		
e)	8	6	48		
f)	10	9	90		

26

5. The question mark (?) is the number we do not know. Write a sentence that gives the unknown.

	Rows	Columns	Total	Sentence
a)	3	5	?	$? = 3 \times 5$
b)	?	6	18	$? = 18 \div 6$
c)	?	2	16	
d)	4	?	36	
e)	7	8	?	
f)	9	?	45	

6. Ken plants 8 rows of trees. He plants 3 trees in each row. How many trees does he plant? Draw an array of dots to show your answer.

7. Randi arranges 35 chairs in rows with 5 chairs in each row. How many rows of chairs does she make?

8. Avril plants 12 flowers in 3 rows. How many flowers are in each row?

9. Mona arranges 9 rows of beads with 7 beads in each row. How many beads are in her array?

BONUS ▶ John makes an array using dimes. He makes 2 rows with 4 dimes in each row.

    a) How many dimes does John use?

    b) If John has 14 dimes in 2 rows, how many dimes are in each row?

BONUS ▶ Marko plants 6 rows of trees with 4 in each row. Tom plants 7 rows of trees with 3 in each row. How many more trees does Marko plant?

BONUS ▶ Wendy arranges 36 stickers with 6 in each row. Raj arranges 49 stickers with 7 in each row. Who has more rows?

NS3-61 Multiplication and Division Word Problems

1. Write two multiplication sentences and two division sentences for the picture.

a)

   _2_ groups

   _3_ in each group

   _6_ in total

   _2 × 3 = 6_

   _3 × 2 = 6_

   _6 ÷ 2 = 3_

   _6 ÷ 3 = 2_

b)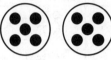

   _____ groups

   _____ in each group

   _____ in total

c)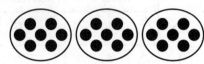

   _____ groups

   _____ in each group

   _____ in total

2. Write two multiplication sentences and two division sentences for each row in the table.

	Number of Groups	Number in Each Group	Total	Sentences	
a)	3	7	21	3 × 7 = 21 7 × 3 = 21	21 ÷ 3 = 7 21 ÷ 7 = 3
b)	9	5	45		
c)	7	6	42		
d)	8	4	32		

3. Write a question mark (?) for the number you do not know.
Then write a sentence that gives the unknown.

	Problem	Number of Groups	Number in Each Group	Total	Sentence
a)	3 pears in each basket 12 pears How many baskets?	?	3	12	? = 12 ÷ 3
b)	4 toys in each box 6 boxes How many toys?				
c)	5 birds on each branch 35 birds How many branches?				
d)	3 children in each boat 12 children in total How many boats?				
e)	3 tents 15 children How many children in each tent?				
f)	5 rows of trees 40 trees How many in each row?				
g)	30 bananas 6 bananas in each bag How many bags?				
h)	9 coins in each pocket 4 pockets How many coins in total?				

4. There are 2 hamsters in each classroom. How many hamsters are in 8 classrooms?

5. Clara bought 24 stamps. There are 8 stamps in each pack. How many packs did she buy?

6. Ronin put 32 granola bars in 8 boxes. He put the same number in each box. How many did he put in each box?

7. Zack bought 8 packs of pens with 5 pens in each pack. Yu bought 9 packs of pens with 4 pens in each pack.

   a) How many pens did Zack buy?

   b) How many pens did Yu buy?

   c) Who bought more pens?

8. Ansel planted 24 flowers with 3 in each row.
Marco planted 42 flowers with 6 in each row.
Who planted more rows?

9. Rani planted 18 trees in 3 rows.
Nina planted 24 trees in 6 rows.
How many more trees are in Rani's rows than in Nina's rows?

10. A chess team has 4 players.
School A sent 20 players to a chess match.
School B sent 32 players to the match.
How many more teams did School B send?

11. A basketball team has 5 players.
School A sent 7 teams to a basketball match.
School B sent 8 teams to the match.
How many players did School A and School B send altogether?

BONUS ▶ An amusement park ride costs 8 tickets. Each car on the ride can seat 3 children.

   12 children want to go on the ride.

   a) How many cars on the ride will the children use?

   b) How many tickets are needed for all the children?

PA3-13 Geometric Patterns

Ronin makes a growing or increasing pattern with squares. He creates a T-table to keep track of the number of squares.

Figure Number	Number of Squares
1	3
2	5
3	7

+2 +2 Add 2 squares each time

The number of squares in the figures makes a growing number pattern: 3, 5, 7.

The rule for the number pattern is "start at 3 and add 2 each time."

1. a) Fill in the T-table for the number of squares in each figure of the geometric pattern. Extend the number pattern.

Pattern A

Figure 1   Figure 2   Figure 3

Figure Number	Number of Squares	
1	4	
2		◯
3		◯
4		◯
5		◯

Pattern B

Figure 1   Figure 2   Figure 3

Figure Number	Number of Squares	
1		
2		◯
3		◯
4		◯
5		◯

b) Write the number pattern and the rule for the number pattern.

A: Number pattern: _____   B: Number pattern: _____

Rule: _____   Rule: _____

_____   _____

c) Ronin has 14 squares. Can he make Figure 5 in each pattern?

A: _____   B: _____

2. a) Fill in the T-table for the number of squares in each figure of the decreasing geometric pattern.

Pattern A

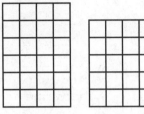

Figure I   Figure 2   Figure 3

Pattern B

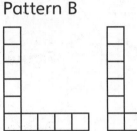 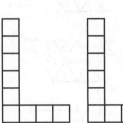

Figure I   Figure 2   Figure 3

Figure Number	Number of Squares
I	
2	
3	

Figure Number	Number of Squares
I	
2	
3	

b) Write the number pattern and the rule for the number pattern.

A: Number pattern: _____

Rule: _____

B: Number pattern: _____

Rule: _____

_____

_____

c) How many squares will be in the next figures of the pattern?

A: Figure 4: _____ squares

Figure 5: _____ squares

Figure 6: _____ squares

B: Figure 4: _____ squares

Figure 5: _____ squares

Figure 6: _____ squares

3. Which number do you add or subtract each time? Write the rule for the number pattern.

a) 10  , 8 , 6 , 4 , 2

Start at _____

b) 2  , 5 , 8 , II , 14

Start at _____

_____

_____

4. Write the rule for the number pattern. On grid paper, sketch a pattern of squares that fits the number pattern. Check by writing a rule for the pattern of squares.

a) 3, 5, 7, 9, II   b) 16, 13, 10, 7, 4   c) I, 5, 9, 13, 17

5. How many shapes are in Figure 6? How do you know?

a) Figure 1

Figure 2

Figure 3

b) Figure 1

Figure 2

Figure 3

c) Figure 1

Figure 2

Figure 3

6. Ella makes a pattern of long rectangles with toothpicks.

Step 1   Step 2   Step 3

a) Make a T-table for the number of toothpicks Ella needs at each step.

b) Ella has 20 toothpicks. How long is the longest rectangle she can make?

7. Jack makes a pattern of rectangles with toothpicks.

Step 1   Step 2   Step 3

a) Make a T-table for the number of toothpicks Jack needs at each step.

b) Jack has 30 toothpicks. How long is the longest rectangle he can make?

BONUS ▶ Make a T-table for the perimeters of Jack's rectangles. What is the perimeter of the longest rectangle Jack can make using 30 toothpicks?

8. Sketch a growing or a shrinking geometric pattern on grid paper. Write the number pattern and the rule for the number pattern.

BONUS ▶ Describe your pattern. How many squares do you add or remove? How do you know where to do that?

PA3-14 Patterns on Number Lines

1. Write the number pattern the picture shows.

a)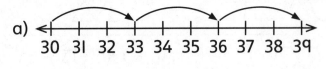

   _30, 33, 36, 39_

b)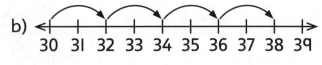

   _____

c)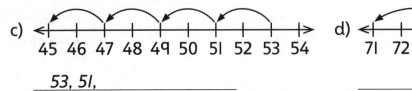

   _53, 51,_ _____

d)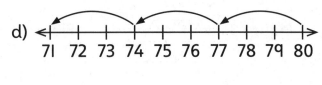

   _____

2. Draw a dot at the start of the number pattern. Write a rule for the number pattern.

a)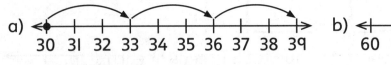

   Start at 30. Add 3 each time.

   _____

b)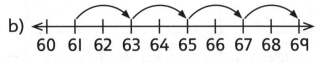

   _____

   _____

c)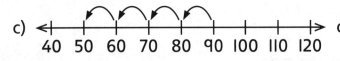

   _____

   _____

d)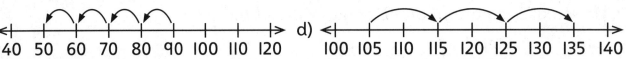

   _____

   _____

e)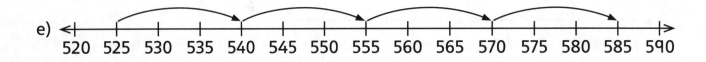

   _____

f)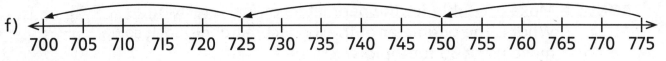

   _____

BONUS ▶

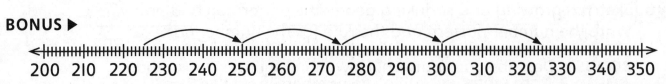

   _____

Patterns and Algebra 3-14

3. Draw dots and arrows to show the pattern on the number line.

a) 30, 32, 34, 36

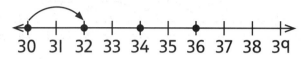

b) 42, 45, 48, 51

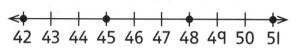

c) 72, 69, 66, 63

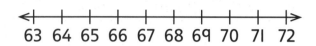

d) 89, 87, 85, 83, 81

4. Write the first 4 numbers in the number pattern. Show the pattern on the number line.

a) Start at 31. Add 2 each time.

_____

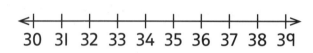

b) Start at 90. Subtract 3 each time.

_____

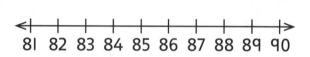

c) Start at 105. Add 5 each time.

_____

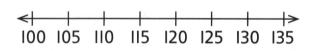

d) Start at 325. Subtract 5 each time.

_____

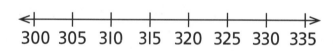

e) Start at 100. Subtract 4 each time. _____

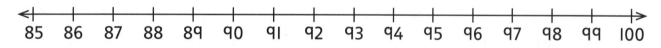

f) Start at 99. Subtract 5 each time. _____

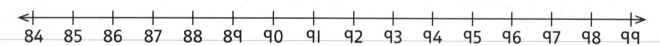

g) Start at 73. Subtract 5 each time. _____

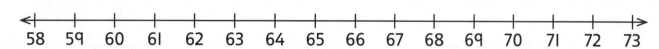

BONUS ▶ Nora writes several more numbers in the pattern
for part g) and gets the number 38. Is she correct? _____

5. a) Draw an increasing pattern on the number line. Write a rule for the number pattern.

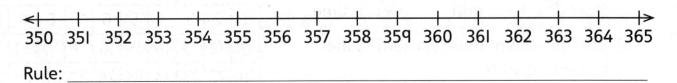

350 351 352 353 354 355 356 357 358 359 360 361 362 363 364 365

Rule: _____

b) Draw a decreasing pattern on the number line. Write a rule for the number pattern.

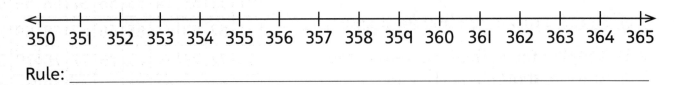

350 351 352 353 354 355 356 357 358 359 360 361 362 363 364 365

Rule: _____

6. a) Write a number pattern for the number of blocks in each figure.

Pattern A

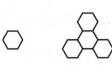

Figure 1   Figure 2   Figure 3

Number pattern: _____

Pattern B

Figure 1   Figure 2   Figure 3

Number pattern: _____

b) Show the number pattern on the number line.

A:

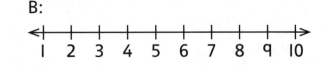

1   2   3   4   5   6   7   8   9   10

B:

1   2   3   4   5   6   7   8   9   10

7. Show the pattern for the number of blocks in each figure on the number line. Use the number line to find how many blocks are in Figure 5.

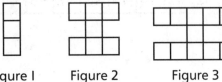

Figure 1   Figure 2   Figure 3

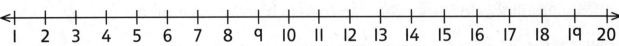

1   2   3   4   5   6   7   8   9   10   11   12   13   14   15   16   17   18   19   20

Figure 5 will have _____ blocks.

PA3-15 Patterns in Charts

1. a) Describe the number pattern in the shaded row.

Start at ______, add ______ each time.

1	2	3	4	5	6	7	8	9	10
11	12	13	14	15	16	17	18	19	20
21	22	23	24	25	26	27	28	29	30
31	32	33	34	35	36	37	38	39	40
41	42	43	44	45	46	47	48	49	50
51	52	53	54	55	56	57	58	59	60
61	62	63	64	65	66	67	68	69	70
71	72	73	74	75	76	77	78	79	80
81	82	83	84	85	86	87	88	89	90
91	92	93	94	95	96	97	98	99	100

b) Describe the number pattern in the shaded column.

____

____

c) Shade a row in the hundreds chart.

d) Describe the number pattern in the row you shaded.

____

____

2. David shades two diagonal patterns of squares on a hundreds chart.

a) Describe the pattern in the light shaded squares.

____

____

b) Describe the pattern in the dark shaded squares.

____

____

1	2	3	4	5	6	7	8	9	10
11	12	13	14	15	16	17	18	19	20
21	22	23	24	25	26	27	28	29	30
31	32	33	34	35	36	37	38	39	40
41	42	43	44	45	46	47	48	49	50
51	52	53	54	55	56	57	58	59	60
61	62	63	64	65	66	67	68	69	70
71	72	73	74	75	76	77	78	79	80
81	82	83	84	85	86	87	88	89	90
91	92	93	94	95	96	97	98	99	100

c) Write nine multiples of 9. Start at 9 and add 9 each time.

____

d) Circle the multiples of 9 on the hundreds chart.

e) Do the multiples of 9 appear in a row, in a column, or on a diagonal? ______________

To count forwards by 5s starting at 4, start at 4 and add 5 each time.

$\overset{+5}{4}, \overset{+5}{9}, \overset{+5}{14}, 19$

To count backwards by 5s starting at 36, start at 36 and subtract 5 each time.

$\overset{-5}{36}, \overset{-5}{31}, \overset{-5}{26}, 21$

3. a) Count forwards by 5s starting at 4. Circle the numbers on the hundreds chart.

   b) Describe the location of the numbers you circled.

   _____

   _____

   c) Write the ones digits of the numbers you circled.

   _____

   d) Describe the pattern in the ones digits.

   _____

1	2	3	4	5	6	7	8	9	10
11	12	13	14	15	16	17	18	19	20
21	22	23	24	25	26	27	28	29	30
31	32	33	34	35	36	37	38	39	40
41	42	43	44	45	46	47	48	49	50
51	52	53	54	55	56	57	58	59	60
61	62	63	64	65	66	67	68	69	70
71	72	73	74	75	76	77	78	79	80
81	82	83	84	85	86	87	88	89	90
91	92	93	94	95	96	97	98	99	100

   e) Karen counts backwards by 5s starting at 94.

   Will she say 39? _____ Will she say 28? _____

4. a) Count forwards by 5s starting at 2. Write 6 numbers. _____

   b) Write the ones digits of the numbers you wrote in part a). _____

   c) Describe the pattern in the ones digits. _____

   d) Describe the pattern in the tens digits. _____

   e) Use the patterns in the ones and the tens digits to write 4 more

   numbers in the pattern. _____

   f) Where are the numbers in the pattern on a hundreds chart?

   _____

   g) Shade the numbers on the hundreds chart in Question 3 to check your answer to part f).

5. a) Count backwards by 5s starting at 93. Write 6 numbers.

_____

b) Predict: If you continue skip counting, will you say 39? _____

Will you say 28? _____ How do you know? _____

_____

6. a) Write four multiples of 7.

$1 \times 7 =$ _____

$2 \times 7 =$ _____

$3 \times 7 =$ _____

$4 \times 7 =$ _____

November

Sun	Mon	Tue	Wed	Thu	Fri	Sat
				1	2	3
4	5	6	7	8	9	10
11	12	13	14	15	16	17
18	19	20	21	22	23	24
25	26	27	28	29	30	

b) Circle the multiples of 7 on the calendar.

c) Describe the locations of the multiples of 7 on the calendar.

_____

d) Shade one row of the calendar. Describe the pattern in the row.

_____

e) Use a different colour to shade a column of the calendar.
Describe the pattern in the column.

_____

7. a) Write five multiples of 6.

$1 \times 6 =$ _____

$2 \times 6 =$ _____

$3 \times 6 =$ _____

$4 \times 6 =$ _____

$5 \times 6 =$ _____

July

Sun	Mon	Tue	Wed	Thu	Fri	Sat
						1
2	3	4	5	6	7	8
9	10	11	12	13	14	15
16	17	18	19	20	21	22
23	24	25	26	27	28	29
30	31					

b) Circle the multiples of 6 on the calendar.

c) Describe the locations of the multiples of 6 on the calendar.

PA3-16 Equal and Not Equal

1. Write the number of balls on each table. Write = if the tables have the same number. Write ≠ if they do not have the same number.

a)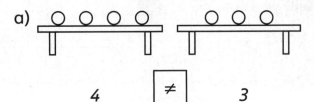

___4___ [≠] ___3___

b)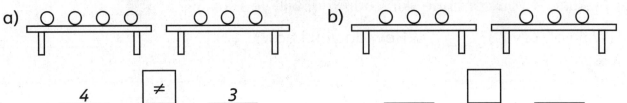

_____ [ ] _____

c)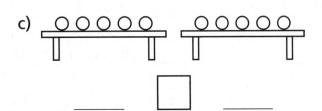

_____ [ ] _____

d)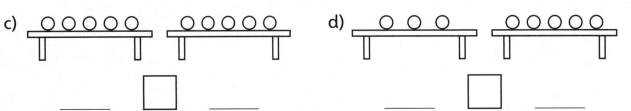

_____ [ ] _____

2. Write the number of balls. Write = or ≠ in the box.

a)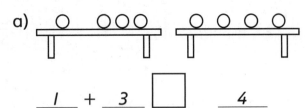

___1___ + ___3___ [ ] ___4___

b)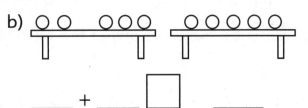

_____ + _____ [ ] _____

c)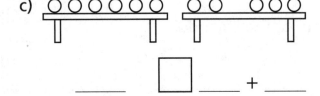

_____ [ ] _____ + _____

d)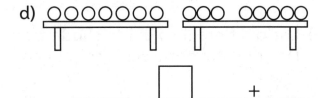

_____ [ ] _____ + _____

e)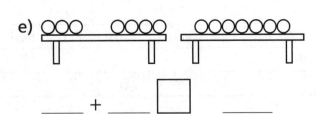

_____ + _____ [ ] _____

f)

_____ + _____ [ ] _____

g)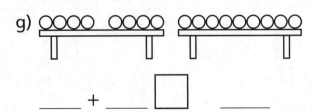

_____ + _____ [ ] _____

h)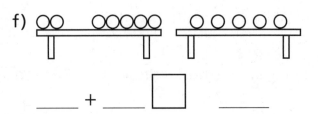

_____ [ ] _____ + _____

3. Circle the correct addition sentence.

a) $\boxed{7 = 3 + 4}$

    $7 \neq 3 + 4$

b) $9 = 5 + 3$

    $\boxed{9 \neq 5 + 3}$

c) $8 = 6 + 2$

    $8 \neq 6 + 2$

d) $5 = 3 + 1$

    $5 \neq 3 + 1$

e) $11 + 5 = 16$

    $11 + 5 \neq 16$

f) $12 + 3 = 15$

    $12 + 3 \neq 15$

An **equation** is a number sentence that has an **equal sign** (=).

    $3 + 5 = 8$

    equal sign

The equal sign shows that the left side of the number sentence has the same value as the right side.

---

4. Circle the number sentences that are equations.

A. $5 + 7 \neq 13$ **B.** $6 < 9$ **C.** $15 - 2 = 13$

D. $4 = 32 \div 8$ **E.** $6 \times 5 > 15$ **F.** $14 \neq 12 + 3$

5. Write "T" if the equation is true. Write "F" if the equation is false.

a) $3 + 7 = 10$ __T__   b) $9 + 4 = 12$ __F__   c) $2 + 17 = 18$ _____

d) $6 - 2 = 4$ _____   e) $24 - 5 = 19$ _____   f) $25 - 13 = 11$ _____

g) $3 \times 9 = 27$ _____   h) $6 \times 7 = 42$ _____   i) $56 = 8 \times 8$ _____

j) $24 \div 4 = 8$ _____   k) $12 \div 3 = 4$ _____   l) $6 = 35 \div 5$ _____

m) $14 + 13 = 27$ _____   n) $9 \times 3 = 28$ _____   o) $9 = 45 \div 5$ _____

p) $18 - 12 = 7$ _____   q) $4 = 15 - 10$ _____   r) $8 = 80 \div 10$ _____

BONUS ▶

s) $2 + 4 = 3 \times 2$ _____   t) $5 + 6 = 14 - 2$ _____   u) $24 \div 6 = 10 - 6$ _____

PA3-17 Addition Equations

1. Some apples are inside the box and some are outside. Draw the missing apples in the box.

   a) [apples] = [apples] + [box with apples]

   total number of apples

   b) [apples] = [apples] + [box]

   c) [apples] + [box] = [apples]

   d) [box] + [apples] = [apples]

   e) [apples] + [apples] = [box]

   f) [box] = [apple] + [apples]

2. Draw the missing apples in the box. Then write the missing number in the smaller box.

   a) [apples] = [apples] + [box with apples]

   5 = 3 + 2

   b) [apples] = [apples] + [box]

   8 = 3 + ☐

   c) [apples] + [box] = [apples]

   3 + ☐ = 4

   d) [box] + [apples] = [apples]

   ☐ + 4 = 7

   e) [apples] + [apples] = [box]

   2 + 4 = ☐

   f) [box] = [apple] + [apples]

   ☐ = 1 + 2

When you find the missing number in the equation, you **solve** it.

3. Draw a picture for the equation. Use your picture to solve the equation.

   a) 5 + ☐ = 6   b) ☐ + 4 = 9

   c) 8 = ☐ + 3   d) ☐ = 4 + 4

To solve ☐ + 3 = 7, Megan guesses the unknown number is 3.

Megan checks her guess. ⟨3⟩ + 3 = 7 is not true.

                           6 is too small. To make a bigger sum, she tries 4.

Megan checks her new guess. ⟨4⟩ + 3 = 7 is true, so the unknown number is 4.

4. Solve the equation by guessing and checking.

   a) ☐ + 3 = 4   b) 2 + ☐ = 9   c) 9 = ☐ + 4   d) 10 = 6 + ☐

   e) 5 + 7 = ☐   f) ☐ = 7 + 6   g) 15 = 9 + ☐   h) ☐ + 8 = 16

You can write 2 addition equations and 2 subtraction equations for this picture.

⬤⬤⬤○○○○

   3 + 4 = 7   4 + 3 = 7   7 − 3 = 4   7 − 4 = 3

These equations make a **fact family**.

5. Write the fact family for the picture.

   a)    b)    c) ○○○○○○⬤

_____   _____   _____

_____   _____   _____

_____   _____   _____

_____   _____   _____

6. Draw a picture for the equation. Write the rest of the fact family.

a) 4 + 2 = 6

2 + 4 = 6, 6 − 2 = 4,

6 − 4 = 2

b) 6 + 1 = 7

_____

_____

c) 6 − 1 = 5

_____

_____

d) 9 − 4 = 5

_____

_____

Some circles are in a box.

There are 8 circles in total. Anton wants to find how many circles are in the box.

He writes the equation 3 + ☐ = 8.

Anton subtracts to find the number of circles in the box: 8 − 3 = 5

7. Draw a picture for the equation. Then write the subtraction to find the missing number.

a) 7 + ☐ = 9

⚫⚫⚫⚫⚫⚫⚫ ☐

9 − 7 = 2

b) 3 + ☐ = 10

_____

c) ☐ + 4 = 8

_____

d) 5 = ☐ + 1

_____

8. Write the subtraction equation to find the missing number.

a) 7 = 4 + ☐

7 − 4 = 3

b) 10 = ☐ + 3

_____

c) ☐ + 6 = 11

_____

d) 10 + ☐ = 19

_____

e) ☐ + 21 = 32   f) 42 + ☐ = 95   g) 69 = ☐ + 14   h) 80 = 36 + ☐

PA3-18 Subtraction Equations

1. Sam takes some apples from a box. Draw the apples that were in the box before.

a)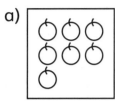

Sam takes away this many   this many are left

b)

c)

d)

2. Draw the missing apples. Then write the missing number in the smaller box.

a)

□ = 5 − 2

b)

6 − □ = 3

c)

4 = 5 − □

d)

7 − 4 = □

3. Draw a picture for the equation. Use your picture to solve the equation.

a) 6 − □ = 1

b) 3 = □ − 6

4. Solve the equation by guessing and checking.

a) $\boxed{} - 2 = 2$ b) $3 = \boxed{} - 4$ c) $8 - 3 = \boxed{}$ d) $\boxed{} = 10 - 2$

e) $9 - \boxed{} = 2$ f) $3 = 10 - \boxed{}$ g) $8 = \boxed{} - 2$ h) $15 - 7 = \boxed{}$

i) $\boxed{} - 8 = 10$ j) $13 = \boxed{} - 4$ k) $28 - 13 = \boxed{}$ l) $7 = \boxed{} - 9$

m) $16 - \boxed{} = 8$ n) $8 = 15 - \boxed{}$ o) $8 = \boxed{} - 6$ p) $20 - \boxed{} = 20$

Lela takes 3 apples from a box. 2 apples are left in the box.

$\boxed{} - 🍎🍎🍎 = 🍎🍎$

$\boxed{} \quad - \quad 3 \quad = \quad 2$

Lela adds the number of apples she took out and the number of apples left to find the number of apples that started in the box.

$3 \quad + \quad 2 \quad = \quad \boxed{5}$

$🍎🍎🍎 + 🍎🍎 = \boxed{🍎🍎🍎🍎🍎}$

---

5. Write an addition equation to find the number of apples that were in the box before.

a) $4 = \boxed{} - 3$ b) $\boxed{} - 1 = 8$ c) $10 = \boxed{} - 3$ d) $6 = \boxed{} - 4$

$\underline{\quad 3 + 4 = 7 \quad}$ $\underline{\qquad\qquad}$ $\underline{\qquad\qquad}$ $\underline{\qquad\qquad}$

e) $\boxed{} - 6 = 6$ f) $\boxed{} - 9 = 4$ g) $9 = \boxed{} - 7$ h) $\boxed{} - 10 = 9$

$\underline{\qquad\qquad}$ $\underline{\qquad\qquad}$ $\underline{\qquad\qquad}$ $\underline{\qquad\qquad}$

i) $\boxed{} - 16 = 6$ j) $\boxed{} - 23 = 14$ k) $19 = \boxed{} - 27$ l) $\boxed{} - 10 = 75$

$\underline{\qquad\qquad}$ $\underline{\qquad\qquad}$ $\underline{\qquad\qquad}$ $\underline{\qquad\qquad}$

m) $\boxed{} - 21 = 32$ n) $\boxed{} - 42 = 40$ o) $61 = \boxed{} - 11$ p) $80 = \boxed{} - 50$

$\underline{\qquad\qquad}$ $\underline{\qquad\qquad}$ $\underline{\qquad\qquad}$ $\underline{\qquad\qquad}$

Patterns and Algebra 3-18

$$2 + 3 = 5, 3 + 2 = 5, 5 - 3 = 2, 5 - 2 = 3$$

6. Write the rest of the equations in the fact family.

a) $6 - 2 = 4,$ _____

b) $10 - 7 = 3,$ _____

7. Write the other subtraction equation from the same fact family.

a) $11 - 3 = 8$ b) $12 - 7 = 5$ c) $17 - 9 = 8$

     $\underline{\quad 11 - 8 = 3 \quad}$ _____   _____

> To find the missing number in $7 - \square = 4$, use $7 - 4 = \square$.
> We know $7 - 4 = 3$, so $7 - \boxed{3} = 4$.

8. Write the other subtraction equation from the same fact family.
Find the number in the box.

a) $7 - \square = 5$ b) $9 - \square = 4$ c) $10 - \square = 2$

     $\underline{\quad 7 - 5 \quad} = \boxed{2}$ $\underline{\qquad\qquad} = \square$ $\underline{\qquad\qquad} = \square$

d) $12 - \square = 5$ e) $14 - \square = 6$ f) $17 - \square = 10$

     $\underline{\qquad\qquad} = \square$ $\underline{\qquad\qquad} = \square$ $\underline{\qquad\qquad} = \square$

g) $32 - \square = 25$ h) $26 = 54 - \square$ i) $17 = 97 - \square$

9. Solve the equation.

a) $\square - 33 = 32$ b) $42 - \square = 40$ c) $71 = \square - 14$

d) $80 = 90 - \square$ e) $\square = 36 - 28$ f) $78 - 29 = \square$

g) $34 = \square - 7$ h) $\square - 40 = 15$ i) $\square = 67 - 39$

BONUS ▶

j) $100 - \square = 51$ k) $71 = \square - 29$ l) $\square - 100 = 0$

PA3-19 Using Letters for Unknown Numbers

You can use a letter to stand for the number you do not know.

Instead of $\boxed{} + 5 = 8$, you can write $x + 5 = 8$ or $a + 5 = 8$.

1. Use x instead of the box. Rewrite the equation.

   a) $\boxed{} + 35 = 70$

   b) $24 = \boxed{} - 6$

   c) $\boxed{} = 7 + 59$

   _____   _____   _____

2. Use y instead of the box. Rewrite the equation.

   a) $45 = 90 - \boxed{}$

   b) $102 = \boxed{} + 6$

   c) $97 - 69 = \boxed{}$

   _____   _____   _____

> **REMINDER ▶** You can use addition   You can use subtraction
> to find the missing total.   to find the missing part.
>
> $x - 5 = 1$ $6 - a = 4$ $2 + y = 8$
>
> $5 + 1 = 6$ $6 - 4 = 2$ $8 - 2 = 6$
>
> $x = 6$ $a = 2$ $y = 6$

3. Solve the equation.

   a) $44 - x = 20$

   $\underline{44 - 20 = 24}$

   $x = \underline{\ 24\ }$

   b) $24 - 6 = n$

   _____

   $n = \underline{}$

   c) $15 = 7 + m$

   _____

   $m = \underline{}$

   d) $y - 28 = 10$

   _____

   $y = \underline{}$

   e) $24 = 6 + b$

   _____

   $b = \underline{}$

   f) $35 = x - 7$

   _____

   $x = \underline{}$

4. How many numbers can you find that solve the equation $\boxed{} + 5 = 12$? Explain.

   _____

   _____

5. Rewrite the equation so there is only one operation. Solve the equation.

a) $25 + 3 = 15 + y$

$28 = 15 + y$

$28 - 15 = 13$

$y = 13$

b) $4 + 24 + n = 70$

c) $x - 10 = 35 + 4$

d) $35 - 10 = b - 15$

e) $p + 12 = 33 - 5$

BONUS ▶ $40 - a = 5 \times 4$

You can also use symbols, such as ☺ or ?, to stand for unknown numbers.
Instead of $\square - 5 = 8$ or $x - 5 = 8$, you can write ☺ $- 5 = 8$ or $? - 5 = 8$.

---

6. Use ☺ instead of a. Rewrite the equation.

a) $44 - a = 20$

b) $25 - 6 = a$

c) $35 = 7 + a$

_____

_____

_____

7. Solve the equation.

a) $? - 8 = 10$

b) $13 = 8 +$ ☆

c) $11 = $ ☺ $- 7$

_____

_____

_____

$? = $ _____

☆ $= $ _____

☺ $= $ _____

d) $29 - ? = 19$

e) $50 = ⟨ + 25$

BONUS ▶ $75 = \bigvee + 75$

_____

_____

_____

$? = $ _____

$⟨ = $ _____

$\bigvee = $ _____

BONUS ▶ Use the same number instead of ☺. Can you find more than one solution to the equation ☺ $+ 0 = $ ☺? Explain.

NS3-62 Equal Paper Folding

In a **fraction**, there are **equal parts** in the whole.

2 equal parts	▭	← Each part is one half.
3 equal parts	▭	← one third
4 equal parts	▭	← one fourth
6 equal parts	▭	← one sixth
8 equal parts	▭	← one eighth

I. Use **paper-folding** to fill in the blanks.

a)

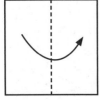

___2___ equal parts

Each part is __*one*__ __*half*__.

b)

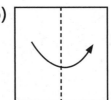

_____ equal parts

Each part is _____ _____.

c)

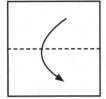

_____ equal parts

Each part is _____ _____.

d)

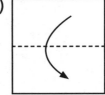 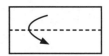

_____ equal parts

Each part is _____ _____.

e)

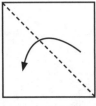

_____ equal parts

Each part is _____ _____.

f)

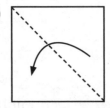 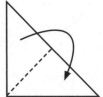

_____ equal parts

Each part is _____ _____.

2. Use paper-folding to fill in the blanks.

a)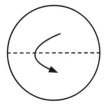

_____ equal parts

Each part is _____ _____.

b)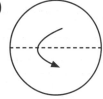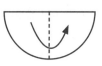

_____ equal parts

Each part is _____ _____.

c)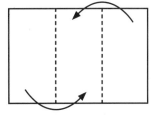

_____ equal parts

Each part is _____ _____.

d)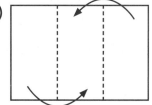

_____ equal parts

Each part is _____ _____.

e)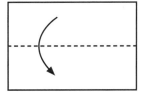

_____ equal parts

Each part is _____ _____.

f)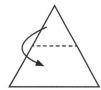

_____ equal parts

Each part is _____ _____.

BONUS ▶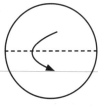

_____ equal parts

Each part is _____ _____.

3. Kyle thinks that each part in the picture is one sixth of the whole. Is he correct? Explain.

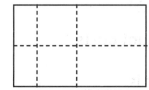

NS3-63 Unit Fractions

There are 4 equal parts.

Each part is one fourth.

One fourth is a fraction.

You can write fractions with words or numbers.

one fourth or $\frac{1}{4}$ ← number of parts shaded
← number of parts in the whole

I. Write the fraction for the equal parts with words and with numbers.

a)

___8___ equal parts

Each part is

___one___ ___eighth___ or $\boxed{\dfrac{1}{8}}$.

b)

_____ equal parts

Each part is

_____ _____ or $\boxed{}$.

c)

_____ equal parts

Each part is

_____ _____ or $\boxed{}$.

d)

_____ equal parts

Each part is

_____ _____ or $\boxed{}$.

e)

_____ equal parts

Each part is

_____ _____ or $\boxed{}$.

f)

_____ equal parts

Each part is

_____ _____ or $\boxed{}$.

A **unit fraction** has only 1 equal part shaded.

2. Write the unit fraction shown by the shaded part of the picture.

a) $\frac{1}{4}$

b)

c)

d)

e)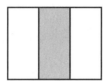

f)

3. Shade the unit fraction.

a) $\frac{1}{5}$

b) $\frac{1}{2}$

c) $\frac{1}{4}$

d) $\frac{1}{10}$

e) $\frac{1}{3}$

f) $\frac{1}{6}$

4. a) Circle the unit fractions.

$\frac{2}{3}$ $\frac{1}{4}$ $\frac{1}{8}$ $\frac{4}{7}$ $\frac{1}{5}$ $\frac{9}{10}$ $\frac{1}{6}$ $\frac{2}{9}$

b) Explain why the fractions that are not circled are not unit fractions.

_____

5. a) Circle the pictures that do not show one fourth.

    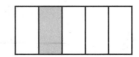

b) Explain why the pictures you circled do not show one fourth.

NS3-64 Writing Fractions

There are 4 equal parts.
3 parts are shaded.

You can write the fraction as $\frac{3}{4}$.

$\frac{3}{4}$ ← The **numerator** tells you 3 parts are shaded.

← The **denominator** tells you 4 parts are in the whole.

1. Count the number of shaded parts and the number of equal parts in the picture. Then write the fraction shown by the shaded parts.

a)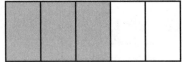

   __3__ shaded parts

   __5__ equal parts

The fraction is $\boxed{\frac{3}{5}}$.

b)

   _____ shaded parts

   _____ equal parts

The fraction is $\boxed{}$.

c)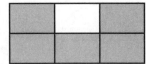

   _____ shaded parts

   _____ equal parts

The fraction is $\boxed{}$.

d)

   _____ shaded parts

   _____ equal parts

The fraction is $\boxed{}$.

2. Write the fraction shown by the shaded part or parts.

a) $\boxed{\frac{2}{5}}$

b) $\boxed{}$

c) $\boxed{}$

d) $\boxed{}$

e) $\boxed{}$

f) $\boxed{}$

3. Shade parts to show the fraction.

a) $\frac{3}{4}$

b) $\frac{2}{3}$

c) $\frac{1}{5}$

d) $\frac{7}{8}$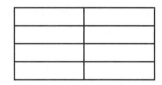

e) $\frac{5}{6}$

f) $\frac{2}{2}$

4. Write a fraction for the parts that are not shaded.

a)

b)

c)

d)

e)

f)

> **REMINDER** ▶ In a fraction, there are equal parts in the whole.

5. Circle the pictures that have equal parts in the whole.

  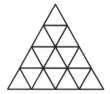 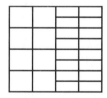

6. a) Circle the picture where the shaded region shows $\frac{2}{3}$.

 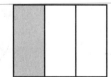

b) For each picture not circled, explain why the shaded region does not show $\frac{2}{3}$.

COPYRIGHT © 2016 JUMP MATH: NOT TO BE COPIED.

7. Write the numerator of the fraction.

a) $\frac{3}{4}$ _____ b) $\frac{5}{8}$ _____ c) $\frac{1}{6}$ _____ d) $\frac{2}{7}$ _____

8. Write the denominator of the fraction.

a) $\frac{7}{8}$ _____ b) $\frac{1}{4}$ _____ c) $\frac{3}{5}$ _____ d) $\frac{5}{6}$ _____

9. You have $\frac{2}{5}$ of a pie.

a) What is the denominator of the fraction? _____

b) What does the denominator tell you? _____

_____

c) What is the numerator of the fraction? _____

d) What does the numerator tell you? _____

_____

10. In Fred's apartment building, $\frac{11}{16}$ of the apartments have people living in them.

a) What is the denominator of the fraction? _____

b) What is the numerator of the fraction? _____

c) How many apartments are in the building? _____

d) How many apartments have people living in them? _____

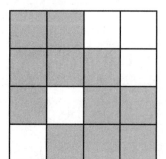

11. On Iva's school bus, $\frac{17}{24}$ of the seats are filled with students.

a) What is the denominator of the fraction? _____

b) What is the numerator of the fraction? _____

c) How many seats are on the bus? _____

d) How many students are seated

on the bus? _____

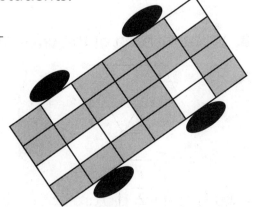

NS3-65 Fractions and Pattern Blocks

These are **pattern blocks** for four shapes.

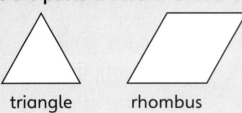 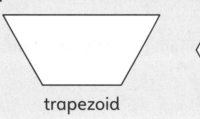 

triangle   rhombus   trapezoid   hexagon

I. a) Which shape has six sides? _____

    b) Which shape has three sides? _____

    c) Which shape has only one pair of parallel sides? _____

    d) Which shape has two pairs of parallel sides? _____

2. a) Connect the dots with a line.
How many triangles cover the rhombus? _____

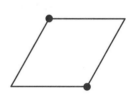

    b) Connect each pair of dots with a line.
How many triangles cover the trapezoid? _____

    c) Draw lines from the point in the centre of
the hexagon to each vertex.

How many triangles cover the hexagon? _____

3. What fraction of the pattern block is the shaded triangle?

a) 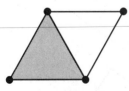   b) 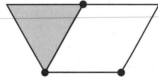   c)

 $\frac{1}{2}$

4. a) What fraction of the hexagon is the trapezoid?

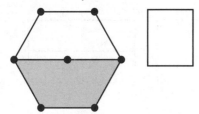

b) What fraction of the hexagon is the rhombus?

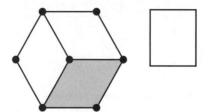

5. What fraction of the picture is shaded?

a)

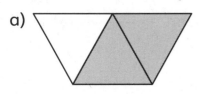

b)

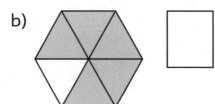

c)

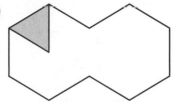

d)

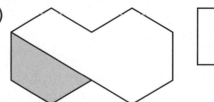

6. What fraction of the picture is shaded?

a)

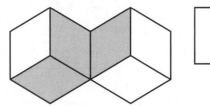

b)

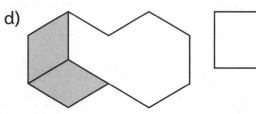

c)

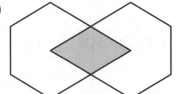

d)

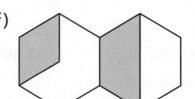

BONUS ▶

e)

f)

I. Shade one half of the shape in two different ways.

a)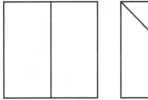

b)

c)

d)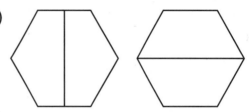

e)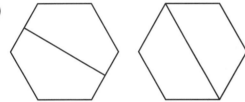

f)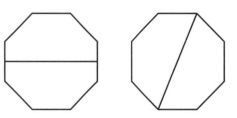

2. Write "yes" or "no" to answer the question for each part in Question I.

a) Are the fractions the same?

b) Do the equal parts look the same?

3. Shade one fourth of the shape in different ways.

a)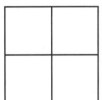

b)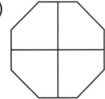

4. Write "yes" or "no" to answer the question for each part in Question 3.

a) Are the fractions the same?

b) Do the equal parts look the same?

5. Add a line to the picture to make 4 equal parts.

a)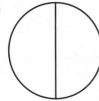

b)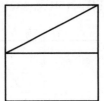

BONUS ▶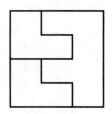

6. Add a line to the picture to make 6 equal parts.

a)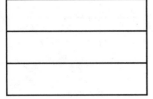

b)

c)

d)

7. Jun must shade in one fifth of the big square.

Is his answer correct? _____

Explain. _____

_____

_____

_____

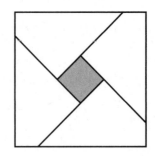

BONUS ▶ Show two different ways to divide a rectangle into 8 equal rectangles.

NS3-67 Different Shapes, Same Fractions

I. Draw a line to create 2 equal parts. Then shade $\frac{1}{2}$ of the whole.

a)

b)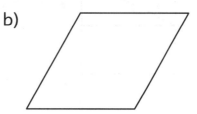

c)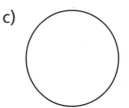

d)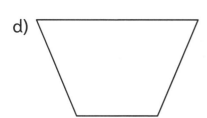

e)

BONUS ▶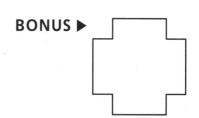

2. Draw a line to create 3 equal parts. Then shade $\frac{2}{3}$ of the whole.

a)

b)

c)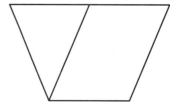

d)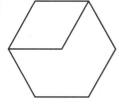

e)

BONUS ▶

3. Draw a line to create 4 equal parts. Then shade $\frac{3}{4}$ of the whole.

a)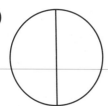

b)

c)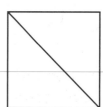

d)

e)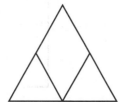

BONUS ▶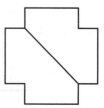

4. One half of a shape is shaded. Outline the whole shape.

a)  b)

c)  d)

e)  f)

g) 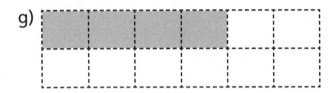 h)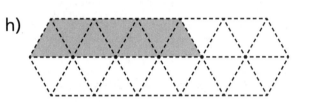

5. One third of a shape is shaded. Outline the whole shape.

a) 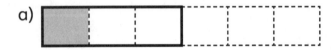 b)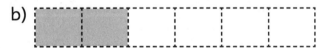

c)  d)

e)  f)

g) 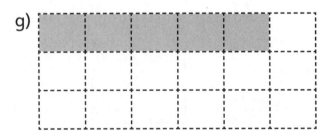 h)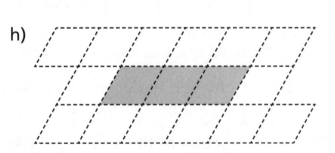

BONUS ▶ One fourth of a shape is shaded. Outline the whole shape.

NS3-68 Fractions of a Set

Fractions can name parts of a set.

There are 5 shapes altogether.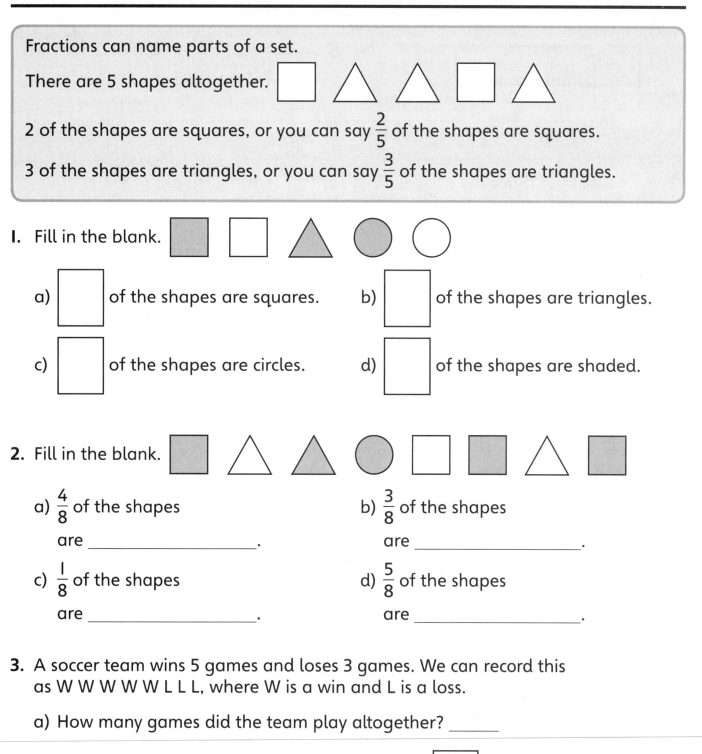

2 of the shapes are squares, or you can say $\frac{2}{5}$ of the shapes are squares.

3 of the shapes are triangles, or you can say $\frac{3}{5}$ of the shapes are triangles.

1. Fill in the blank.

   a) ☐ of the shapes are squares.

   b) ☐ of the shapes are triangles.

   c) ☐ of the shapes are circles.

   d) ☐ of the shapes are shaded.

2. Fill in the blank.

   a) $\frac{4}{8}$ of the shapes

      are _____.

   b) $\frac{3}{8}$ of the shapes

      are _____.

   c) $\frac{1}{8}$ of the shapes

      are _____.

   d) $\frac{5}{8}$ of the shapes

      are _____.

3. A soccer team wins 5 games and loses 3 games. We can record this as W W W W W L L L, where W is a win and L is a loss.

   a) How many games did the team play altogether? _____

   b) What fraction of the games did the team win? ☐

   c) What fraction of the games did the team lose? ☐

4. Write four fraction statements for the picture.

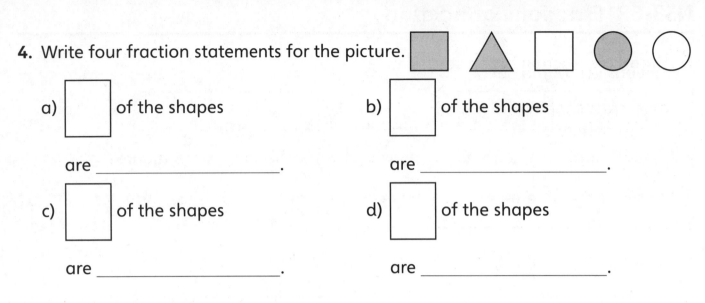

a) ⬜ of the shapes

are _____.

b) ⬜ of the shapes

are _____.

c) ⬜ of the shapes

are _____.

d) ⬜ of the shapes

are _____.

5. Draw a picture that fits all the statements.

a) There are 5 circles and squares. $\frac{3}{5}$ of the shapes are squares.

$\frac{2}{5}$ of the shapes are shaded. Two circles are shaded.

b) There are 5 triangles and squares. $\frac{3}{5}$ of the shapes are shaded.

$\frac{2}{5}$ of the shapes are triangles. One square is shaded.

6.

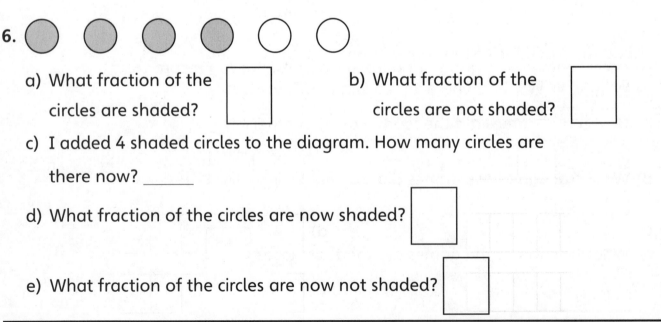

a) What fraction of the circles are shaded? ⬜

b) What fraction of the circles are not shaded? ⬜

c) I added 4 shaded circles to the diagram. How many circles are there now? _____

d) What fraction of the circles are now shaded? ⬜

e) What fraction of the circles are now not shaded? ⬜

NS3-69 Comparing Fractions

1. Shade the fraction of the strip.

a) 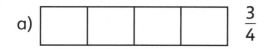 $\frac{3}{4}$

b)  $\frac{2}{3}$

c) 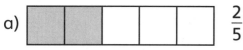 $\frac{2}{5}$

d)  $\frac{7}{8}$

2. Which strip has more shaded? Circle the greater fraction.

a)  $\frac{2}{5}$

$\frac{3}{5}$

b) 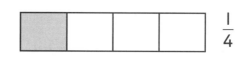 $\frac{3}{4}$

$\frac{1}{4}$

c) 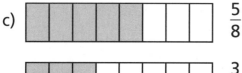 $\frac{5}{8}$

$\frac{3}{8}$

d)  $\frac{1}{3}$

$\frac{2}{3}$

To compare fractions, the wholes must be the same.

$\frac{7}{8}$ is greater than $\frac{3}{8}$ because more of the whole is shaded.

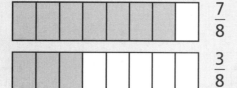 $\frac{7}{8}$

$\frac{3}{8}$

3. Shade the fractions of the strips. Then circle the greater fraction.

a) 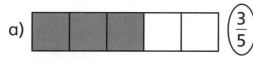 $\frac{3}{5}$

$\frac{2}{5}$

b) 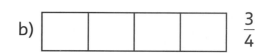 $\frac{3}{4}$

$\frac{1}{4}$

c) 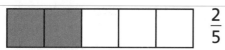 $\frac{5}{8}$

$\frac{7}{8}$

d) 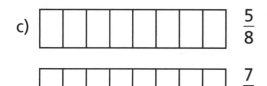 $\frac{3}{6}$

$\frac{5}{6}$

4. Shade the fractions of the strips. Then circle the smaller fraction.

a) 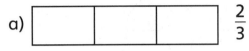 $\frac{2}{3}$

$\frac{1}{3}$

b) 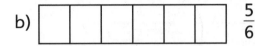 $\frac{5}{6}$

$\frac{6}{6}$

c) 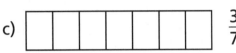 $\frac{3}{7}$

$\frac{6}{7}$

d)  $\frac{0}{4}$

$\frac{1}{4}$

"5 is greater than 3" is written as 5 > 3.　　　"3 is less than 5" is written as 3 < 5.

5. Circle the greater fraction. Then use the correct sign (< or >) to compare the fractions.

a) 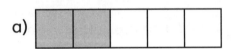 $\frac{2}{5}$

$\left(\frac{3}{5}\right)$

$\frac{2}{5}$ < $\frac{3}{5}$

b) 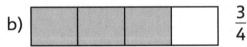 $\frac{3}{4}$

$\frac{1}{4}$

$\frac{3}{4}$ ☐ $\frac{1}{4}$

c) 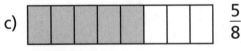 $\frac{5}{8}$

$\frac{3}{8}$

$\frac{5}{8}$ ☐ $\frac{3}{8}$

d) 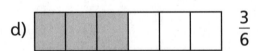 $\frac{3}{6}$

$\frac{5}{6}$

$\frac{3}{6}$ ☐ $\frac{5}{6}$

6. Jessica looked at the pictures and said that $\frac{1}{3} > \frac{2}{3}$. Explain her mistake.

$\frac{1}{3}$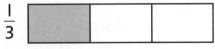

$\frac{2}{3}$

7. Find the circle that has more shaded. Circle the greater fraction.

a)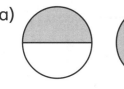

$\frac{1}{2}$ $\frac{2}{3}$

b)

$\frac{3}{4}$ $\frac{1}{3}$

8. Shade the fraction of the circle. Circle the smaller fraction.

a)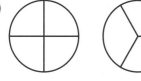

$\frac{1}{4}$ $\frac{1}{3}$

b)

$\frac{6}{8}$ $\frac{4}{6}$

9. Circle the larger fraction. Then use the correct sign (< or >) to compare them.

a)

$\frac{1}{4}$ $\frac{1}{6}$

b)

$\frac{2}{3}$ $\square$ $\frac{7}{8}$

10. Lily and Ed have two pizzas of equal size. Lily ate two thirds of her pizza. Ed ate three quarters of his pizza. Which fraction is bigger? Who ate more?

     $\frac{2}{3}$ $\square$ $\frac{3}{4}$ _____ ate more.

11. John thinks he has more pizza than Mary because $\frac{3}{4} > \frac{1}{2}$. Is he correct? Explain.

John   Mary

NS3-70 Fraction Squares

1. Count on by the unit fraction.

a) $\frac{1}{4}$, $\frac{2}{4}$, ☐ , ☐

b) $\frac{1}{5}$, $\frac{2}{5}$, ☐ , ☐ , ☐

c) $\frac{1}{3}$, ☐ , ☐

d) $\frac{1}{2}$, ☐

2. Write a fraction for the shaded part of the circle. Then count on by the fraction to count all the equal parts of the circle.

a)

$\frac{1}{4}$ | $\frac{2}{4}$ | $\frac{3}{4}$ | $\frac{4}{4}$

b) ☐

☐ ☐ ☐

c) ☐

☐ ☐ ☐ ☐ ☐

d) ☐

☐ ☐

3. Write a fraction for the shaded part of the square. Then count on by the fraction to count all the equal parts of the square.

a) ☐

☐ ☐ ☐ ☐

b) ☐

☐ ☐ ☐ ☐

c) ☐

☐ ☐

d) ☐

☐ ☐

Two half squares cover the same area as one whole square.

You can circle pairs of half squares to find the area.

  Area = 2 squares

4. Find the total area, in squares, by circling pairs of half squares.

a)  _____ squares

b)  _____ squares

c)  _____ squares

d)  _____ squares

5. Find the area of the shaded parts by counting the whole squares and half squares.

a)  _____ squares

b)  _____ squares

c) 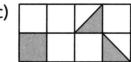 _____ squares

d)  _____ squares

6. Find the area of the shaded parts by counting whole squares and half squares.

a) 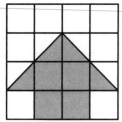 _____ squares

b) 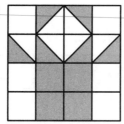 _____ squares

BONUS ▶ 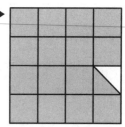 _____ squares

ME3-14 Digital Clocks

> **Digital clocks** show both the hours and the minutes with two digits. The digital clock shows that 5 minutes have passed after 3 o'clock.
>
> We say the time is 3:05 or 5 minutes past 3.
>
> **03:05**
> hours   minutes

1. Write the time in numbers.

a)

___2:17___

b) **12:20**

_____

c) **01:03**

_____

2. Write the time in words and numbers.

a)

___15 minutes past 7___

_____

b) **10:20**

_____

_____

c) **01:23**

_____

_____

d)

_____

_____

e) **02:40**

_____

_____

f) **06:09**

_____

_____

3. Write the time the way it looks on a digital clock.

a) 7:01

| 0 | 7 | : | 0 | 1 |

b) 4:15

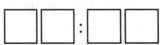

c) 3:08

d) 4 minutes past 9

e) 12 minutes past 12

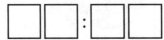

f) 9 minutes past 11

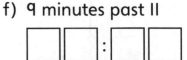

g) 23 minutes past 2

h) 30 minutes past 6

i) 1 minute past 2

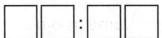

ME3-I5 Analog Clock Faces and Hands

Analog clock faces show numbers from I to I2 in a circle.
An analog clock has different hands.

The **hour hand** is shorter.

The **minute hand** is longer.

minute hand→
hour hand⟶

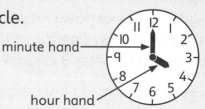

I. Which hand is shaded, the hour hand or the minute hand?

a)
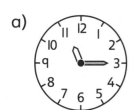
hour   (minute)

b)
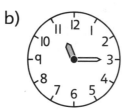
hour   minute

c)
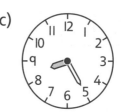
hour   minute

d)
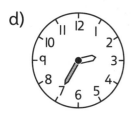
hour   minute

e)
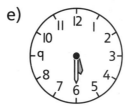
hour   minute

f)

hour   minute

g)
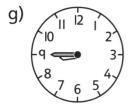
hour   minute

h)
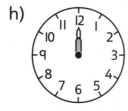
hour   minute

i)
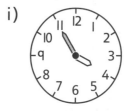
hour   minute

j)
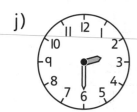
hour   minute

k)
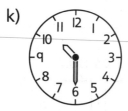
hour   minute

l)
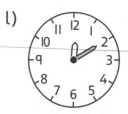
hour   minute

2. How is an analog clock face the same as a number line? How is it different from a number line?

The minute hand points directly at 12.
The hour hand points directly at 3.
The time is 3 **o'clock**.

We write this time as 3:00.

3. Draw a line to show where the hour hand is pointing. Is it o'clock?
Write "yes" or "no."

a)

_____

b)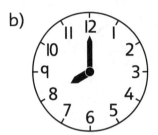

_____

c)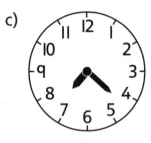

_____

4. What time is it?

a)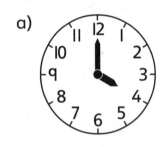

    __4__ : 00

    __4 o'clock_____

b)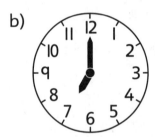

    _____ : 00

_____

c)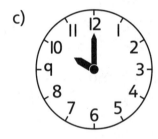

    _____ : 00

_____

d)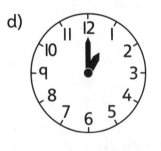

    _____ : 00

_____

e)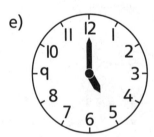

    _____ : 00

_____

f)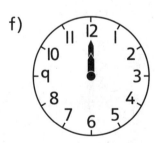

    _____ : 00

_____

Measurement 3-15

Both hands move from one number to the next.

When the hour hand points between the numbers
7 and 8, the hour is still 7.

5. Draw a line from the hour hand. Write the hour.

a)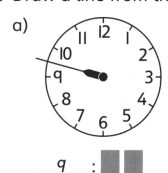

___9___ : ▮▮

b)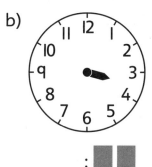

_____ : ▮▮

c)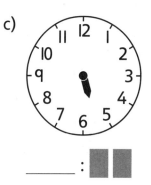

_____ : ▮▮

6. Circle the hour hand. Then write the hour.

a)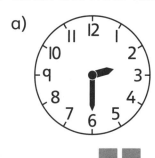

_____ : ▮▮

b)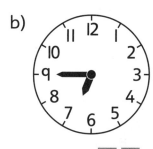

_____ : ▮▮

c)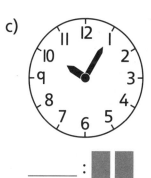

_____ : ▮▮

d)

_____ : ▮▮

e)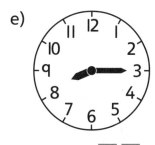

_____ : ▮▮

f)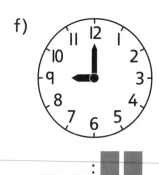

_____ : ▮▮

BONUS ▶ The numbers on the clock faces are missing! Match the clock to the time.

a) 5:00 _____

b) 9:00 _____

A.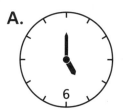

B.

ME3-16 The Minute Hand

When the minute hand moves from one number on the clock face to the next, 5 minutes have passed.

How many minutes is it past 9:00? Count by 5s.

1. How many minutes is it past 9:00? Count by 5s.

a)

___25___ minutes

b)

_____ minutes

c)

_____ minutes

d)

_____ minutes

e)

_____ minutes

f)

_____ minutes

2. Rob thinks that the time is 9:05 because the minute hand points at 5.

Explain his mistake. _____

_____

_____

_____

3. Circle the minute hand. Then count by 5s to write the minutes.

a)

2 : __30__

b)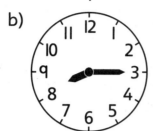

8 : _____

c)

10 : _____

d)

9 : _____

e)

1 : _____

f)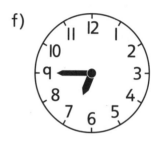

6 : _____

g)

11 : _____

h)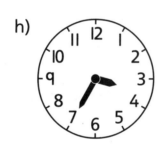

3 : _____

i)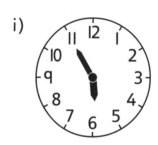

5 : _____

4. What time is it?

a)

_____ minutes past 12

b)

_____ minutes past 4

c)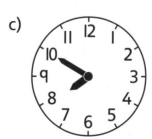

_____ minutes past 7

Measurement 3-16

75

The minute hand points at 3. Three times 5 minutes have passed after 9:00.

3 × 5 = 15 minutes have passed. The time is 9:15.

5. Draw the arrows to show how the minute hand moved from 9:00. Then write the multiplication equation.

a)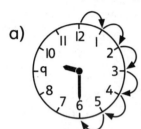

   _____6 × 5 = 30_____

b)

   _____

c)

   _____

d)

   _____

e)

   _____

f)

   _____

6. Write a multiplication equation for the minutes passed after 9:00. Then write the time.

a)

   _____7 × 5 = 35_____

   9 : _35_

b)

   _____

   9 : _____

c)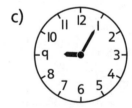

   _____

   9 : _____

✎ BONUS ▶ The minute hand made one whole circle. How many minutes passed? How do you know?

ME3-17 Time to the Five Minutes

What time is it?

Step 1: Look at the hour hand. It points between 4 and 5.
The hour is 4.

Step 2: Look at the minute hand. It points at 2. Skip count by 5s
or multiply by 5 to find the minutes: 5, 10, or 2 × 5 = 10.

The time is 4:10.

1. What time is it?

a)

____1____ : ____40____

b)

_____ : _____

c)
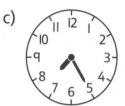

_____ : _____

d)
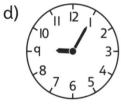

_____ : _____

e)
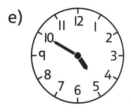

_____ : _____

f)
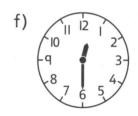

_____ : _____

2. Write the time on the digital clock.

a)
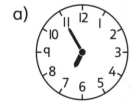

0 6 : 5 5

b)
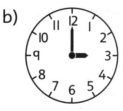

☐☐ : ☐☐

c)
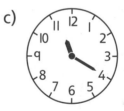

☐☐ : ☐☐

d)
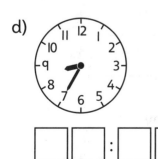

☐☐ : ☐☐

e)

☐☐ : ☐☐

f)
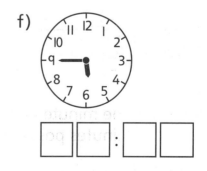

☐☐ : ☐☐

3. Write the time two ways.

a)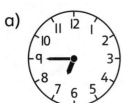

_6:45_

forty-five

minutes past six

b)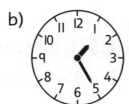

_____

_____

_____

c)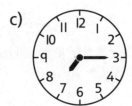

_____

_____

_____

d)

_____

_____

_____

e)

_____

_____

_____

f)

_____

_____

_____

g)

_____

_____

_____

h)

_____

_____

_____

i)

_____

_____

_____

BONUS ▶

a) Show the time 7:05 on the analog and the digital clock.

b) Write the time in words.

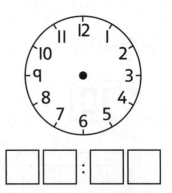

_____

_____

Measurement 3-17

ME3-18 Half and Quarter Hours

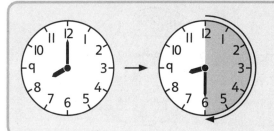

It is half an hour after 8:00.
The time is **half past** 8.

$6 \times 5 = 30$, so the time is 8:30.

1. Write the time two ways.

a)

half past _____

_____ : _____

b)

half past _____

_____ : _____

c)

half past _____

_____ : _____

d)

half past _____

_____ : _____

2. Write the time in numbers.

a) half past 8   b) half past 6   c) half past 10   d) half past 12

_____   _____   _____   _____

Some digital clocks do not show the first zero in the hours.
The clock shows half past 2.

3. Write the time in words and numbers.

a) 7:30

_half past 7_____

b) 9:30

_____

c) 12:30

_____

d) 1:30

_____

e) 10:30

_____

f) 5:30

_____

4. What fraction of the circle is shaded?

a)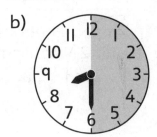

_____

b)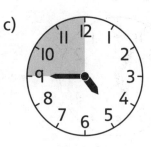

_____

c)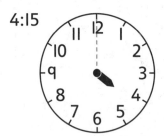

_____

5. a) Draw the minute hand on each clock. How much after the hour is it? Show by colouring.

7:15

4:15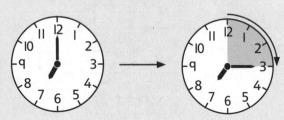

12:15

b) What fraction of each circle did you colour? _____

c) What fraction of an hour is 15 minutes? _____

It is a quarter of an hour after 7:00 or **quarter past** 7.
$3 \times 5 = 15$, so the time is 7:15.

6. Write the time in words and numbers. Use "quarter" in your answer.

a)

_____

_____

b)

_____

_____

c)

_____

_____

7. Write the time in words. Use "half," "quarter," and "o'clock" when you can.

a)

_____fifty-five minutes_____

_____past six_____

b)

_____half past twelve_____

_____

c)

_____

_____

d)

_____

_____

e)

_____

_____

f)

_____

_____

g)

_____

_____

h)

_____

_____

i)

_____

_____

j)

_____

_____

k)

_____

_____

l)

_____

_____

📓 **BONUS ▶** Write the time in as many ways as you can.

a)

b)

c)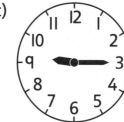

ME3-19 Minutes to the Hour

The hour hand is between 6 and 7.

How many minutes are left before 7 o'clock?

The minute hand is at 9.

Count by 5s to get from 12 to 9: 5, 10, 15.

The time is 15 minutes **to** 7.

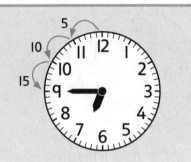

1. What time is it?

a)

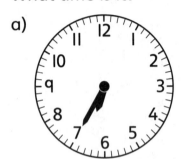

__25__ minutes to 7

b)

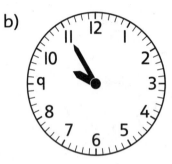

_____ minutes to 10

c)

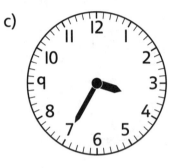

_____ minutes to 4

d)

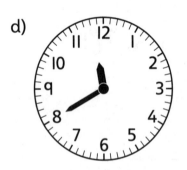

_____ minutes to _____

e)

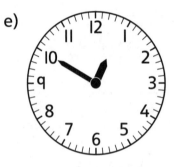

_____ minutes to _____

f)

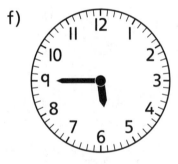

_____ minutes to _____

g)

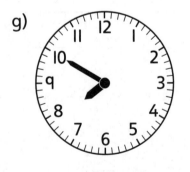

_____ minutes to _____

h)

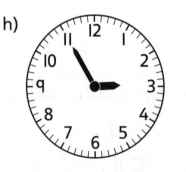

_____ minutes to _____

i)

_____ minutes to _____

2. Tell the time two ways, as minutes past the hour and minutes
to the next hour.

a)

_____ minutes past _____

_____ minutes to _____

b)

_____ minutes past _____

_____ minutes to _____

c)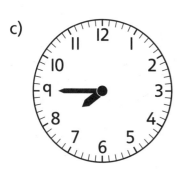

_____ minutes past _____

_____ minutes to _____

d)

_____ minutes past _____

_____ minutes to _____

It is 4:40. How much time is left before 5 o'clock?
There are 60 minutes in 1 hour. 40 minutes passed after 4:00.

60 − 40 = 20 minutes left

The time is 20 minutes to 5.

---

3. How many minutes are left before 5 o'clock? Write the subtraction equation.

a) 4:37

60 − _37_

= _23_

b) 4:05

60 − _____

= _____

c) 4:50

60 − _____

= _____

d) 4:58

60 − _____

= _____

e)

_____

f)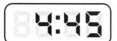

_____

g)

_____

h)

_____

4. Tell the time two ways.

a) `11:58`

_____ minutes past _____

_____ minutes to _____

b) `10:35`

_____ minutes past _____

_____ minutes to _____

c) `5:30`

_____ minutes past _____

_____ minutes to _____

d) `4:16`

_____ minutes past _____

_____ minutes to _____

Three quarters of an hour passed after 4:00. One quarter of an hour is left before 5:00.

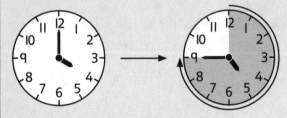 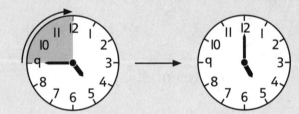

The time is **quarter to** 5.

5. What time is it? Use "quarter to" in your answer.

a)

b)

c)

___*quarter to 1*___   _____   _____

d) `1:45`   e) `4:45`   f) `7:45`

6. Write the time in words in as many ways as you can.

a) 6:12   b) 7:15   c) 3:00   d) 12:45   e) 10:30   f) 2:35

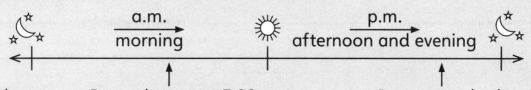

Use **a.m.** to show times from 12:00 midnight to 11:59.

Use **p.m.** to show times from 12:00 noon to 11:59.

Examples: Jay wakes up at 7:00 a.m.   Jay goes to bed at 9:15 p.m.

1. Write "a.m." or "p.m."

a) Lily eats breakfast at 7:30 _____   b) Ray goes to school at 8:15 _____

c) School ends at 3:35 _____   d) Dinner is at 5:30 _____

e) Karate class starts at 5:45 _____   f) The math test starts at 9:15 _____

2. Write the time. Use "a.m." or "p.m."

a) The morning TV show starts at

_____6:45 a.m._____

b) The bedtime story ends at

_____

c) Hanna eats lunch at

_____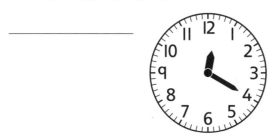

d) Anton gets to school at

_____

e) Half past 8 in the morning is

_____

f) Quarter past 5 in the evening is

_____

BONUS ▶

g) 3 hours before noon is

_____

h) 12 minutes after midnight is

_____

Timelines are like number lines for time. They can show times or events in order.

3. Fill in the missing times on the timeline.

a)

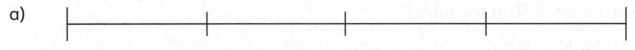

8:00 a.m.   _8:15 a.m._   _8:___ a.m._   _____   9:00 a.m.

b)

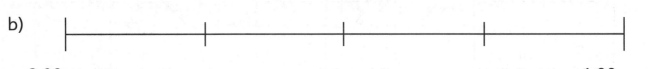

3:00 p.m.   _____   _____   _____   4:00 p.m.

4. The timeline shows what Jun does after school.

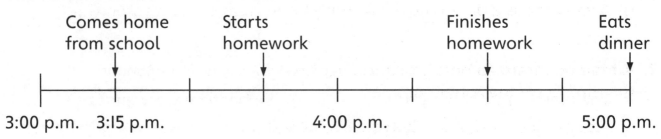

Comes home from school   Starts homework   Finishes homework   Eats dinner

3:00 p.m.   3:15 p.m.   4:00 p.m.   5:00 p.m.

a) Use Jun's timeline to fill in the table. Use "a.m." and "p.m."

Event	Time
Comes home from school	
Starts homework	
Finishes homework	

b) How much time does homework take? _____

c) How much time does he have after homework and before dinner? _____

d) Jun's dad comes home from work 15 minutes before dinner.

At what time does Jun's dad come home? _____

Show this time on the timeline.

BONUS ▶ Is the time that passed from the time Jun starts homework to dinner more than 1 hour or less than 1 hour? How do you know?

ME3-21 Intervals of Time

| I week = 7 days | I day = 24 hours | I hour = 60 minutes |

1. Skip count to fill in the table.

a)
Weeks	Days
I	
2	
3	

b)
Days	Hours
I	
2	
3	

c)
Hours	Minutes
I	
2	
3	

2. a) Nina's birthday is in 2 weeks. How many days until Nina's birthday? _____

   b) A weekend is 2 days long. How many hours long is one weekend? _____

3. A train ride from Toronto to Vancouver takes 87 hours. How long is
   the trip? Circle the correct answer.

   between 2 and 3 days   between 3 and 4 days   between 4 and 5 days

4. A test is 90 minutes long.

   a) Is the test longer than I hour? _____

   b) Is the test longer than 2 hours? _____

5. Ronin walks his dog 3 times a day, 20 minutes each time.

   a) How many minutes does he walk his dog in one day? _____

   b) How many hours does he walk his dog in one day? _____

   c) How many hours each week does Ronin spend walking his dog? _____

6. Zara exercises 40 minutes every day.

   a) How many minutes does she exercise in one week?

   Hint: Skip count by 40. _____

   b) A doctor says Zara should exercise at least 3 hours a week.

   Does she exercise enough? _____

7. Multiply by 7 to convert weeks to days. Add the leftover days.

a) 2 weeks 3 days

    2 weeks = __14__ days

    2 weeks 3 days

    = __14 + 3__ days

    = __17__ days

b) 3 weeks 2 days

    3 weeks = _____ days

    3 weeks 2 days

    = _____ days

    = _____ days

c) 4 weeks 5 days

    4 weeks = _____ days

    4 weeks 5 days

    = _____ days

    = _____ days

d) 1 week 5 days

    = _____ days

    = _____ days

e) 3 weeks 6 days

    = _____ days

    = _____ days

f) 5 weeks 1 day

    = _____ days

    = _____ days

BONUS ▶ Circle the time periods in Question 7 that are longer than 1 month.

8. Change the hours to minutes. Add the leftover minutes.

a) 2 hours 3 minutes

    = __120 + 3__ minutes

    = __123__ minutes

b) 3 hours 20 minutes

    = _____ minutes

    = _____ minutes

c) 4 hours 15 minutes

    = _____ minutes

    = _____ minutes

d) 1 hour 55 minutes

e) 3 hours 30 minutes

f) 5 hours 1 minute

9. Tom reads a book for 1 hour 45 minutes. Kathy reads a book for 115 minutes. Who spends more time reading? How much longer does this person read?

10. There are 52 weeks in 1 year.

a) Iva is exactly 2 years old. How many weeks old is Iva?

b) Lewis is 42 weeks old. Nora is 30 weeks older than Lewis. Who is older, Nora or Iva? Explain.

c) Marcel is 6 weeks younger than Iva. Who is older, Nora or Marcel? Explain.

11. A decade is 10 years long. A century is 100 years long. A millennium is 1000 years long. If a ones block represents 1 year, what do the other base ten blocks represent?

ME3-22 Units of Time

I minute = 60 seconds

1. a) Fill in the table.

Minutes	I	2	3	4	5	6
Seconds	60					

b) Ava runs for 3 minutes. How many seconds does she run for? _____

2. Change the minutes to seconds. Add the leftover seconds.

a) 2 minutes 7 seconds

= __120 + 7__ seconds

= __127__ seconds

b) 3 minutes 40 seconds

= _____ seconds

= _____ seconds

c) 4 minutes 23 seconds

= _____ seconds

= _____ seconds

d) I minute 57 seconds

= _____ seconds

= _____ seconds

e) 6 minutes 10 seconds

= _____ seconds

= _____ seconds

f) 5 minutes 5 seconds

= _____ seconds

= _____ seconds

3. Bill can run 500 m in I minute 50 seconds. Ethan can run 500 m in 103 seconds. Who can run 500 m faster? _____

4. What unit of time would you use in the answer? Choose from seconds, minutes, hours, days, months, and years.

a) How long is your favourite TV show? _____

b) How old are you? _____

c) How long is the school day? _____

d) How long does it take you to run 100 m? _____

e) How long is March Break? _____

f) How long is the summer vacation? _____

g) How long ago did Nunavut become a territory? _____

h) How long does it take you to do 10 jumping jacks? _____

i) How long is one half of a soccer game? _____

5. Does the activity take less than 1 minute or more than 1 minute?

a) eating breakfast

_____

b) blinking 10 times

_____

c) brushing your teeth

_____

d) watering a plant

_____

e) going to school

_____

f) playing a hockey game

_____

6. Does the activity take less than 1 hour or more than 1 hour?

a) eating lunch

_____

b) sleeping at night

_____

c) brushing your teeth

_____

d) making a bed

_____

e) getting dressed

_____

f) the school day

_____

7. Use a calendar to fill in the tables.

Month	Number of Days
January	
February	
March	
April	

Month	Number of Days
May	
June	
July	
August	

Month	Number of Days
September	
October	
November	
December	

8. a) Jennifer's birthday is on July 23. Luc's birthday is 10 days after Jennifer's. When is Luc's birthday?

b) Kate's birthday is on April 20. Glen's birthday is 2 weeks later. When is Glen's birthday?

c) Sandy's birthday is 3 weeks before Kate's. When is Sandy's birthday?

BONUS ▶ It takes about 15 minutes to walk 1 km.

a) Will walking 5 km take less than 1 hour, about 1 hour, or more than 1 hour?

b) About how many kilometres can you walk in 1 hour?

ME3-23 Capacity

1. Circle the bottle with more liquid.

a)  b)  c)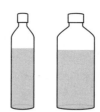

2. Circle the glass with less liquid.

a)  b)  c)

3. Circle the container with more liquid.

a)

b)

c)

BONUS ▶ Circle the container with the most liquid.

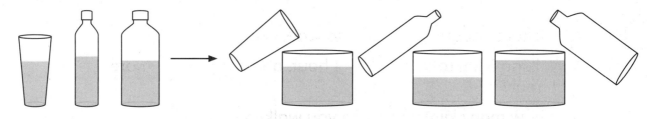

4. Circle the container that holds more.

a)

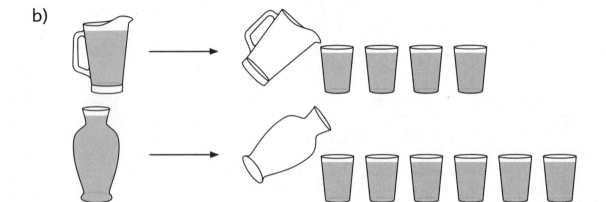

b)

5. Circle the container that holds less.

a)

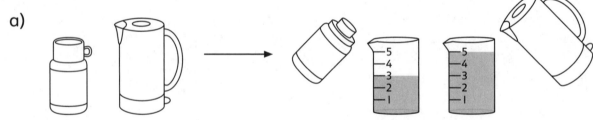

b)

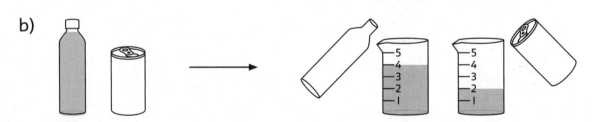

BONUS ▶ Circle the container that holds more.

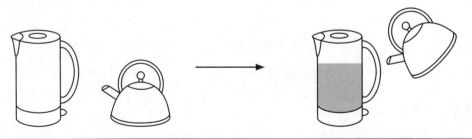

The **capacity** of a container is how much it can hold.

6. Circle the container that has a greater capacity.

a)

b)

c)

Capacity is measured in **litres**. We write **I L** for I litre.

A tall, thin carton holds I L of milk or juice.

7. The milk carton has a capacity of I L. Estimate the capacity of the other container.

a)

Capacity = _____ L

b)

Capacity = _____ L

c)

Capacity = _____ L

The **volume** of a liquid is how much space it takes up.

The container has a capacity of 3 L.

The water in the container has a volume of 2 L.

8. Find the capacity of the container and the volume of the liquid.

a)

Capacity = _____ L

Volume = _____ L

b)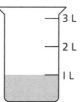

Capacity = _____ L

Volume = _____ L

c)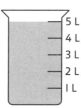

Capacity = _____ L

Volume = _____ L

9. Estimate the capacity in litres. Use a I L bottle to measure the capacity.

a) a bucket

b) a large jug

c) a large milk carton

d) a container of your choice

ME3-24 Fractions of a Litre

1. Draw lines to match containers that have about the same capacity.

> 2 halves make 1 whole.
>
> 2 containers of $\frac{1}{2}$ L fill a 1 L container.
>

2. Jasmin has a 1 L carton of milk. She fills $\frac{1}{2}$ L cartons with milk from the 1 L carton. Fill in the table.

All small cartons full?	yes		
Room left in small cartons?	no		
Milk left in 1 L carton?	yes		

3. Eddy has a 1 L carton of juice. He tries to fill 2 containers with juice from the carton. Write ✓ to show what is true.

a)

☐ bottles full

☐ juice left in carton

b)

☐ bottles full

☐ juice left in carton

c)

☐ containers full

☐ juice left in carton

4. Circle the containers that have a capacity of about one half of a litre.

5. Order the containers by capacity from smallest (1st) to largest (3rd).
   Write "1st," "2nd," and "3rd."

a)

Container	Capacity	Order
small water bottle	$\frac{1}{2}$ L	
paint can	4 L	
tall milk carton	1 L	

b)

Container	Capacity	Order
pail	8 L	
pop can	$\frac{1}{2}$ L	
large juice carton	2 L	

4 quarters or 4 fourths make 1 whole.

A glass has a capacity of $\frac{1}{4}$ L. 4 glasses of $\frac{1}{4}$ L fill a 1 L container.

6. Each small carton has a capacity of one fourth of a litre. Match the
   picture to the description.

A.   B.   C.

a) less than 1 L _____   b) exactly 1 L _____   c) more than 1 L _____

7. Order the containers by capacity from largest (1st) to smallest (6th).

$\frac{1}{2}$ L   1 L   4 L $\frac{1}{4}$ L   2 L   20 L

_____   _____   _____   _____   _____   _____

8. Tess has a 1 L carton of juice. She tries to fill 4 containers with juice
   from the carton. Write ✓ to show what is true.

a)

[✓] glasses full

[ ] juice left in carton

b)

[ ] bottles full

[ ] juice left in carton

c)

[ ] containers full

[ ] juice left in carton

9. Circle the containers that have a capacity of about one fourth of a litre.

10. a) What fraction of the set of glasses is full?

A.    **B.**    **C.**

b) Each glass has a capacity of $\frac{1}{4}$ L. How many litres can all 4 glasses hold together?

A: ___*I L*___   B: _____   C: _____

c) What is the total volume of juice in each set?

A: $\frac{1}{4}$ L   B: C:

11. Find the capacity of the container and the volume of the juice.

a)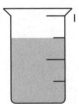

Capacity = ___*I L*___

Volume = $\frac{3}{4}$ L

b)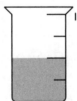

Capacity = _____

Volume =

c)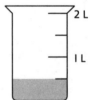

Capacity = _____

Volume =

d)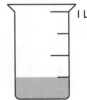

Capacity = _____

Volume =

e)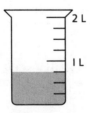

Capacity = _____

Volume =

f)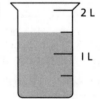

Capacity = _____

Volume =

12. Choose a container that can hold less than I L. Estimate and measure its capacity in fractions of a litre.

> **Mass** is the amount of matter in an object.
>
> The heavier the object, the greater the mass.

I. Circle the object that has more mass.

a)

b)

c)

2. Circle the object that has less mass.

a)

b)

c)

> A **balance** is used to find if two objects have the same mass.
>
> equal   heavier   lighter

3. Circle the heavier object.

a)

b)

c)

d)

e)

f)

4. Circle the lighter object.

a)    b)    c)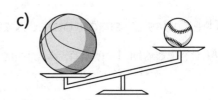

5. Circle the heavier object. Hint: Use what the balance tells you.

a)     b)

c)      d)

6. Circle the heavier object. Hint: Use what the balances tell you.

a)

b)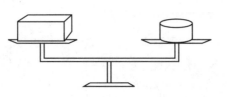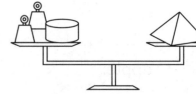

BONUS ▶ Circle the heaviest object.

ME3-26 Grams and Kilograms

> The mass of small objects can be measured in **grams**.
> Write **I g** for I gram. A large paper clip weighs about I g.

1. Circle the objects that have a mass of about I g each.

2. Draw lines to match objects that weigh about the same.

> A tennis ball weighs about 50 g.   A small potato weighs about I00 g.

3. Circle the objects that have a mass of I00 g or more. Draw an X
   on the objects that have a mass less than 50 g.

4. What is the mass of the object?

a)

Mass of apple:

about _____ g

b)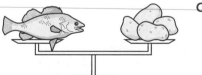

Mass of fish:

about _____ g

c)

Mass of I mitten:

about _____ g

We use a **scale** to measure mass.

5. Estimate the mass of the object in grams. Use a scale to measure the mass.

   a) a 25¢ coin

   Estimate: _____

   Mass: _____

   b) large scissors

   Estimate: _____

   Mass: _____

   c) a calculator

   Estimate: _____

   Mass: _____

   d) a notebook

   Estimate: _____

   Mass: _____

   e) an object of your choice: _____

   Estimate: _____

   Mass: _____

We measure the mass of larger objects in **kilograms**.

Write **I kg** for I kilogram. A tall, thin carton of milk has a mass of I kg.

6. Circle the objects that have a mass of about I kg each.

7. Estimate the mass of the object in kilograms. Use a scale to measure the mass.

   a) a stack of books

   Estimate: _____

   Mass: _____

   b) a backpack

   Estimate: _____

   Mass: _____

   c) a student

   Estimate: _____

   Mass: _____

   d) a laptop

   Estimate: _____

   Mass: _____

   e) an object of your choice: _____

   Estimate: _____

   Mass: _____

I kg = 1000 g

8. Circle the larger mass.

   a) 300 g   3 kg

   b) I kg   999 g

   c) 1000 g   10 kg

9. Circle the best unit for measuring the mass of the object.

a)

g   kg

b)

g   kg

c)

g   kg

d)

g   kg

10. Write the missing mass needed to make the balance level.

a)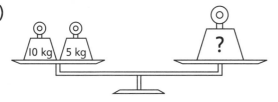

? = _____

b)

? = _____

11. Circle the better estimate for the mass of the object.

a)

100 g   100 kg

b)

800 g   800 kg

c)

10 g   10 kg

d)

3 g   3 kg

e) a pen cap

1 g   1 kg

f) 2 footballs

1 g   1 kg

g) 4 apples

1 g   1 kg

h) 3 chocolate chips

1 g   1 kg

12. Order the animals from heaviest to lightest.

_____

_____

Animal	Mass
Black bear	110 kg
Chipmunk	50 g
Pacific salmon	4 kg
Puffin	750 g

13. Megan and Lewis each made a tower from cubes.

a) Lewis thinks that because Megan's tower is taller, it has a larger mass. Is he correct? Explain.

b) Megan's tower weighs 18 g. How much does Lewis's tower weigh? Explain.

Megan's tower

Lewis's tower

ME3-27 Mass Word Problems

1. Mandy's granola bar has 3 g of protein.

   How much protein is in 6 granola bars? _____

2. A grape weighs 6 g.

   a) What is the mass of 4 grapes? _____

   b) What is the mass of 10 grapes? _____

   BONUS ▶ What is the mass of 100 grapes? _____

3. There are 5 boxes in a delivery truck. All the boxes weigh the same.
   The total mass of the boxes is 35 kg. What is the mass of each box? _____

4. Don piles boxes with masses of 54 kg, 32 kg, 26 kg, and 75 kg on a cart.

   a) What is the total mass of the boxes? _____

   b) The cart can carry at most 200 kg. What is the greatest mass of

   a box that Don can add to the cart? _____

5. John, Sun, Mike, and Yu balance a see-saw. John
   weighs 28 kg. Sun weighs 23 kg. Mike weighs 27 kg.
   How much does Yu weigh? Show your work.

   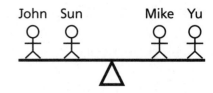

6. Cam goes on a plane trip. Luggage is free if it weighs 23 kg or less.
   Cam's luggage weighs 27 kg.

   a) How much over the limit is Cam's luggage? _____

   b) The company charges 20 dollars for each kilogram over 23 kg.

   How much does Cam have to pay for his luggage? _____

7. A bag of cement weighs 25 kg.

a) How much do 2 bags of cement weigh? _____

b) How much do 4 bags of cement weigh? _____

c) How much do 8 bags of cement weigh? _____

8. 32 lentils weigh 8 g.

a) How much do 64 lentils weigh? _____

b) How much do 16 lentils weigh? _____

c) How many lentils weigh 1 g? _____

BONUS ▶ How many lentils weigh 100 g? _____

9. The mass of 200 ants is 1 g.

a) How many ants have a mass of 2 g altogether?

b) How many ants have a mass of 3 g altogether?

BONUS ▶ What is the mass of 800 ants?

10.

Animal	Mass of Animal	Mass of Food Eaten in a Day
Gerbil	85 g	10 g
Syrian hamster	195 g	20 g
Fancy mouse	40 g	5 g
Meadow vole	44 g	24 g

a) How much food does a hamster eat in 3 days?

b) How much food does a gerbil eat in 1 week?

c) Lynn has 27 grams of mouse food. Does she have enough to feed her pet mouse for 5 days? Show how you know.

d) How much heavier is a gerbil than a vole? How much more food does a vole eat in 2 days than a gerbil eats in 2 days?

e) What is the mass of a mouse? How many days will it take a mouse to eat the amount of food equal to its mass?

11. Jen says that her dog weighs 10 L. Is this correct? Explain.

ME3-28 Fractions of a Kilogram

1. Would 2 of the given item have a mass of about 1 kg?
   Write "yes" or "no."

   a) apple _____   b) soccer ball _____   c) JUMP Math book _____

   2 halves make 1 whole.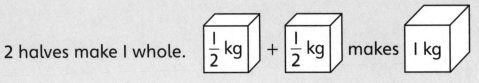

2. Circle the objects that weigh about one half of a kilogram.
   Draw an X on the objects that weigh more than 1 kg.

3. Would 4 of the given item have a mass of about 1 kg?
   Write "yes" or "no."

   a) apple _____   b) soccer ball _____   c) cup of water _____

   4 quarters or 4 fourths make 1 whole.

   $\frac{1}{4}$ kg + $\frac{1}{4}$ kg + $\frac{1}{4}$ kg + $\frac{1}{4}$ kg makes 1 kg

4. Circle the objects that weigh about one fourth of a kilogram.
   Draw an X on the objects that weigh less than one fourth of a kilogram

5. Will the balance be level? Write "yes" or "no."

   a)    b)    c)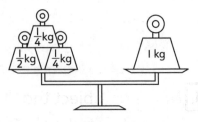

6. Fill in the numbers.

a) 6 is double __3__, so __3__ is half of 6.

b) 8 is double _____, so _____ is half of 8.

c) 10 is double _____, so _____ is half of 10.

d) 100 is double _____, so _____ is half of 100.

e) 1000 is double _____, so _____ is half of 1000.

f) 1 kg = 1000 g, so one half of 1 kg = _____ g.

1 kg = 1000 g	$\frac{1}{2}$ kg = 500 g	$\frac{1}{4}$ kg = 250 g	$\frac{3}{4}$ kg = 750 g

7. Lela measured the mass of the object. About what fraction of a kilogram does the object weigh?

a) tomato
225 g $\boxed{\frac{1}{4} kg}$

b) book
496 g $\boxed{}$

c) watermelon
770 g $\boxed{}$

d) water bottle
523 g $\boxed{}$

e) phone
241 g $\boxed{}$

f) canoe paddle
729 g $\boxed{}$

8. Estimate the mass as a fraction of a kilogram. Measure the mass.

a) a book

Estimate:

Mass:

b) an apple

Estimate:

Mass:

c) a shoe

Estimate:

Mass:

d) a water bottle

Estimate:

Mass:

e) an object of your choice: _____

Estimate:

Mass:

9. Name an object that has the given mass.

a) about $\frac{1}{4}$ kg

b) about $\frac{1}{2}$ kg

c) about $\frac{3}{4}$ kg

ME3-29 Temperature

We use a **thermometer** to check how hot or cold something is.

The hotter the object, the higher its **temperature**.

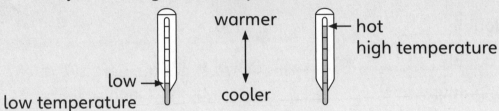

1. Circle the glass with warmer water.

a)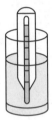

b)

c)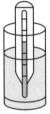

2. Circle the thermometer that shows a lower temperature.

a)

b)

BONUS ▶

In Canada, we measure temperature in **degrees Celsius**.

A thermometer shows each degree with a line.
The thermometer on the right shows 50 degrees Celsius.

Write **50°C** for 50 degrees Celsius.

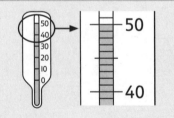

3. The picture shows part of a thermometer. What temperature does the thermometer show?

a)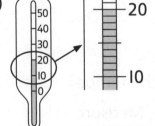

b)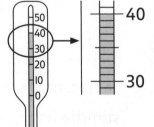

c)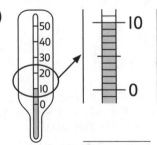

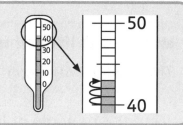

Count the degrees up from the last multiple of 10 to the level of the colour.

The colour reaches 3 degrees above 40°C.
The thermometer shows 43°C.

4. The picture shows part of the thermometer. What temperature does the thermometer show?

a)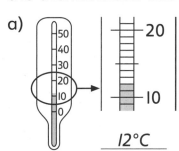

   12°C

b)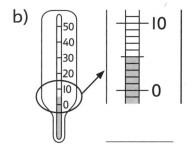

   _____

c)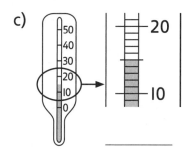

   _____

d)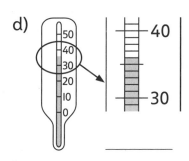

   _____

e)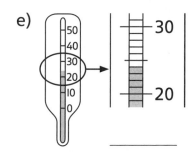

   _____

f)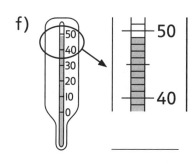

   _____

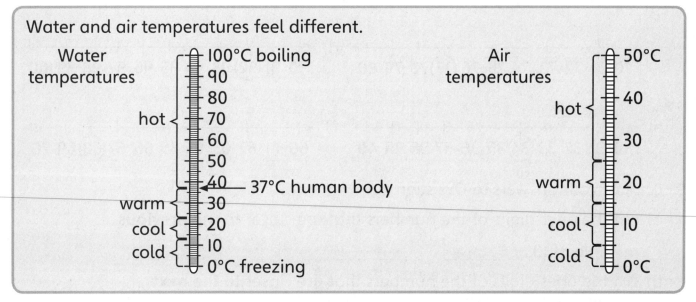

Water and air temperatures feel different.

5. a) Estimate the temperature in your classroom. Measure the temperature.

   b) Pour some water into a glass. Estimate its temperature. Measure the temperature of the water.

NS3-71 Rounding Tens

Multiples of 10 are the numbers you say when counting by tens starting at 0.
0, 10, 20, 30, 40, 50, 60, 70, 80, 90, 100, and so on.

1. Find the multiple of 10 that comes after the number.

   a) 23, __30__   b) 64, _____   c) 78, _____   **BONUS ▶** 101, _____

2. Find the multiple of 10 that comes before the number.

   a) __40__, 46   b) _____, 85   c) _____, 22   **BONUS ▶** _____, 109

3. Find the multiples of 10 before and after the number.

   a) __40__, 43, __50__   b) _____, 67, _____   c) _____, 18, _____

   d) _____, 71, _____   e) _____, 7, _____   f) _____, 35, _____

4. Draw an arrow to show if the circled number is closer to the
   multiple of 10 that comes before or after the number.

   a) 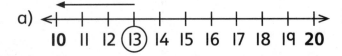   b)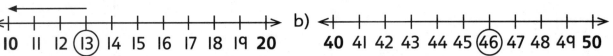

   c) 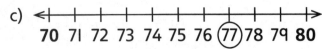   d)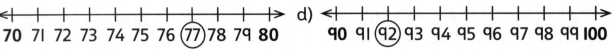

   e) 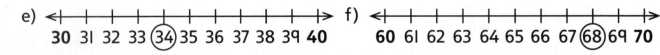   f)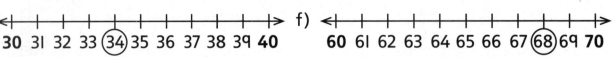

5. Look at your answers to Question 4.

   a) List the ones digits of the numbers that are closer to the **previous**

      multiple of 10. _____

   b) List the ones digits of the numbers that are closer to the **next**

      multiple of 10. _____

   c) Why are the numbers with a ones digit of 5 a special case?

      _____

When **rounding** to the nearest multiple of 10:

- if the ones digit is 1, 2, 3, or 4, **round down** to the previous multiple of 10.
- if the ones digit is 5, 6, 7, 8, or 9, **round up** to the next multiple of 10.

Examples: 53 rounds down to 50.   47 rounds up to 50.

6. Round to the nearest multiple of 10. Circle the answer.

a) 58 is rounded to   50   or   ⟨60⟩

b) 32 is rounded to   30   or   40

c) 64 is rounded to   60   or   70

d) 21 is rounded to   20   or   30

e) 77 is rounded to   70   or   80

f) 25 is rounded to   20   or   30

7. Find the previous and the next multiple of 10. Which would you round the number to? Circle it.

a) 27   __20__   or   ⟨_30_⟩

b) 43   _____   or   _____

c) 89   _____   or   _____

d) 65   _____   or   _____

e) 14   _____   or   _____

f) 7   _____   or   _____

8. Round to the nearest ten.

a) 62 | 60 |

b) 47 | |

c) 39 | |

d) 21 | |

9. Simon has 87 baseball cards. Rounded to the nearest ten, how many baseball cards does he have? _____

10. Tessa's mother worked 43 hours last week. Rounded to the nearest ten, how many hours did she work? _____

11. Jack picked 76 cherries for his basket. Rounded to the nearest ten, how many cherries did he pick? _____

NS3-72 Estimating

1. Round to the nearest ten.

   a) 14 ☐   b) 28 ☐   c) 72 ☐

   d) 39 ☐   e) 17 ☐   f) 45 ☐

2. Round to the nearest ten, then add or subtract.

   a)   52 → | 50 | b)   19 → | ☐ | c)   47 → | ☐ |
      + 34 → + | 30 | + 65 → + | | − 34 → − | |
              | 80 |

When you round numbers to the nearest ten and then calculate, you **estimate** the answer.

3. Estimate by rounding each number to the nearest ten.

   a) 32 + 28   b) 74 − 33   c) 39 + 25

   ___30 + 30 = 60___   _____   _____

   d) 59 − 41   e) 37 + 28   f) 68 − 29

   _____   _____   _____

   BONUS ▶

   g) 23 + 37 + 17   h) 59 − 21 + 48   i) 48 − 21 − 12

   _____   _____   _____

4. Students collected donated coats. Round each number to the nearest ten. Add to estimate the answer.

  a) Cody collected 34 coats and Ava collected 23 coats. How many coats did they collect altogether?

  b) Shelly collected 86 coats and Jin collected 18 coats. How many coats did they collect altogether?

5. Students collected books to raise money for charity. Round each number to the nearest ten to estimate the difference between the numbers collected.

  a) Nina collected 58 books. David collected 43 books.

  b) Marcel collected 84 books. Alexa collected 72 books.

6. Kathy brought 46 muffins to school for a bake sale. Josh brought 37 muffins. Estimate the total number of muffins by rounding each number to the nearest ten.

7. There are 76 cars parked in the front parking lot of the arena. There are 39 cars parked in the rear parking lot. Round each number to the nearest ten to estimate how many more cars are parked in the front parking lot than in the rear parking lot.

8. During a food drive, Sandy's class brought in the number of cans shown in the table. Round each number to the nearest ten to estimate the total number of cans brought in for the week.

Monday	Tuesday	Wednesday	Thursday	Friday
19	21	11	28	14

9. Eddy's father travels a total of 19 km each weekday to go to work and return home. Estimate the total distance he travels from Monday to Friday using addition.

  BONUS ▶ Use multiplication to estimate the total distance he travels in a week.

NS3-73 Estimating Quantities

You can estimate the number of dots in the picture by counting the number of groups of 10.

The first group of 10 is called a **referent**.

There are about three other groups with the same number of dots as the referent.

So you can estimate that the picture has about 4 × 10 = 40 dots.

1. Using 10 as a referent, outline the other groups. Estimate the number of squares in the picture.

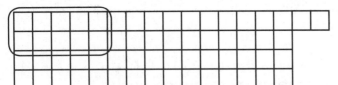

The number of squares is about

_____ × 10 = _____

2. Ten jelly beans are shaded. Use the shaded referent to estimate the number of jelly beans in the jar.

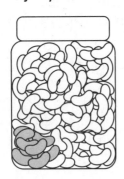

The number of jelly beans is about

_____ × 10 = _____

3. Ten sticks are shaded. Use the shaded referent to estimate the total number of sticks.

The number of sticks is about

_____ × 10 = _____

When there are many more than 100 things in a group, use 100 as a referent instead of 10.

100 dots are circled in the picture.

Sara circles 4 other groups of about 100 dots. She estimates that the picture has about 5 × 100 = 500 dots.

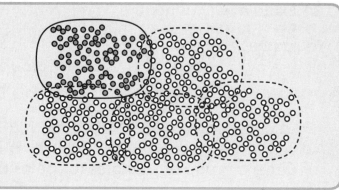

4. Using 100 as a referent, estimate the total number of sticks.

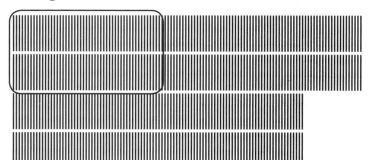

The number of sticks is about

_____ × 100 = _____

5. Using 100 as referent, estimate the total number of stars.

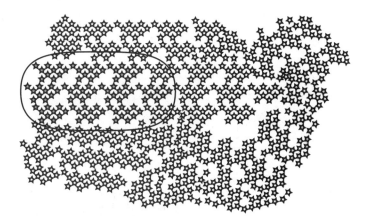

The number of stars is about

_____ × 100 = _____

6. Circle about 100 dots. Use it as a referent to count the total number of dots.

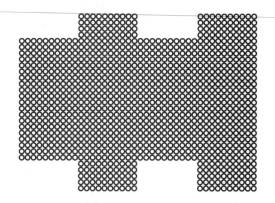

The number of dots is about

_____ × 100 = _____

7. a) Explain why using 10 as a referent
for counting the number of triangles
in the picture is a good choice.

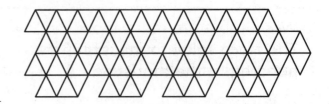

_____

_____

b) Circle a group of triangles to use as a referent.

c) Circle the best estimate of the total number of triangles.

       8   800   80

8. Edmond wants to estimate the number of people
running in a race. He takes a picture of all the
contestants from above. He thinks there are
at least 500 people in the race.

a) About how many people should he circle
in the picture to use as a referent? Explain
your answer.

_____

b) He circles 9 groups of people altogether. About how many
people are in the race? Explain your answer.

_____

9. Dory wants to estimate the number of people
watching her school football game. She takes
a picture of the stands. She thinks there are
fewer than 100 people sitting in the stands.

a) About how many people should she circle
in the picture to use as a referent? Explain
your answer.

_____

b) She circles 7 groups of people altogether. About how many
people are in the stands? Explain your answer.

_____

NS3-74 Place Value: Ones, Tens, Hundreds, and Thousands

> The place value to the left of the hundreds is the **thousands**.
>
>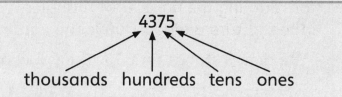

1. Write the place value of the underlined digit.

   a) 3564 _tens_

   b) 1336 _____

   c) 256 _____

   d) 1230 _____

   e) 3859 _____

   f) 5745 _____

2. Underline the digit 3, then write its place value.

   a) 3640 _thousands_

   b) 347 _____

   c) 431 _____

   d) 2413 _____

   e) 1237 _____

   f) 3645 _____

> **REMINDER ▶** You can also write numbers by using a place value chart.
>
> Example: 4375
>
> | Thousands | Hundreds | Tens | Ones |
> |-----------|----------|------|------|
> | 4 | 3 | 7 | 5 |

3. Write the number by using the place value chart.

		Thousands	Hundreds	Tens	Ones
a)	3287	3	2	8	7
b)	9021				
c)	485				
d)	36				
e)	3221				
f)	5602				

The number 2836 is a **4-digit number**.

- The **digit** 2 stands for 2000. The **value** of the digit 2 is 2000.
- The digit 8 stands for 800. The value of the digit 8 is 800.
- The digit 3 stands for 30. The value of the digit 3 is 30.
- The digit 6 stands for 6. The value of the digit 6 is 6.

4. Write the value of each digit.

a)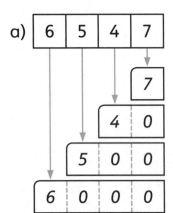

b)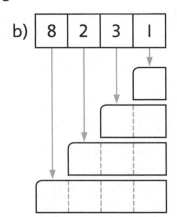

c)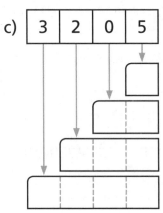

5. What does the digit 3 stand for in the number?

a) 632   [30]

b) 6325   [   ]

c) 6231   [   ]

d) 4305   [   ]

e) 6732   [   ]

f) 3092   [   ]

g) 5321   [   ]

h) 2003   [   ]

i) 1238   [   ]

6. Fill in the blanks.

a) In the number 6572, the digit 5 stands for _____.

b) In the number 4236, the digit 3 stands for _____.

c) In the number 8021, the value of the digit 8 is _____.

d) In the number 2387, the digit _____ is in the tens place.

e) In the number 3729, the value of the digit 7 is _____.

f) In the number 9845, the digit _____ is in the thousands place.

NS3-75 Adding to Make a 4-Digit Number

Sometimes the sum of two 3-digit numbers is a 4-digit number.

Example: 862 + 631

8 hundreds + 6 tens + 2 ones	862
6 hundreds + 3 tens + 1 one or	+ 631
14 hundreds + 9 tens + 3 ones	1493

after regrouping   1 thousand + 4 hundreds + 9 tens + 3 ones

1. Add the numbers.

a)
	3	8	5
+	9	1	1

b)
	4	2	3
+	6	1	4

c)
	8	6	0
+	5	3	0

d)
	2	1	7
+	9	7	0

e)
	3	8	2
+	8	1	6

f)
	1	1	5
+	8	2	1

g)
	6	3	6
+	4	4	0

h)
	9	1	2
+	9	1	7

i)
	6	2	5
+	8	0	2

2. Add. You might need to regroup once or twice.

a)
		3	6	5
	+	4	2	5

b)
		2	3	1
	+	9	8	3

c)
		8	2	3
	+	5	4	7

3. Add. You might need to regroup three times.

a)
	2	8	2
+	8	4	1

b)
	6	5	3
+	4	8	9

c)
	8	0	2
+	9	1	8

4. Write the numbers in the grid. Then add.

a) 282 + 510

b) 627 + 932

c) 512 + 739

5. Amy ran very fast for 518 seconds, then jogged slowly for 623 seconds. How many seconds did she run altogether?

6. A construction company built two apartment buildings. One building has 734 apartments. The other building has 293 apartments. How many apartments did the company build altogether?

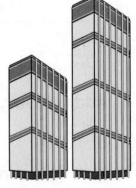

BONUS ▶ Add or subtract.

a)
```
  2875
+ 3121
_____
```

b)
```
  4281
+ 3814
_____
```

c)
```
  3821
-  210
_____
```

d)
```
  4523
- 3109
_____
```

e) 4732 + 3859

f) 4891 − 2193

①	2	3	4	5	⑥	7	8	9	10
⑪	12	13	14	15	16	17	18	19	20
21	22	23	24	25	26	27	28	29	30
31	32	33	34	35	36	37	38	39	40

1. a) Skip count by 5s starting at 1.

___*1*___ , ___*6*___ , ___*11*___ , _____, _____, _____, _____, _____

b) Circle the ones digits in the answers to part a). What pattern

do you see? _____

2. There are some patterns when you skip count by 5s. Underline the
ones digit in each number. Write the pattern in the ones digits.

a) 1<u>2</u>, 1<u>7</u>, 2<u>2</u>, 2<u>7</u>, 3<u>2</u>, 3<u>7</u>   Pattern in the ones digits: _____, _____, _____, _____

b) 14, 19, 24, 29, 34, 39 Pattern in the ones digits: _____, _____, _____, _____

c) 13, 18, 23, 28, 33, 38 Pattern in the ones digits: _____, _____, _____, _____

3. Skip count by 5s to complete the pattern.

a) 23, 28, ___*33*___, _____, _____, _____   b) 34, 39, _____, _____, _____, _____

c) 45, 50, _____, _____, _____, _____   d) 16, 21, _____, _____, _____, _____

4. Skip count backwards by 5s to complete the pattern.

a) 48, 43, ___*38*___, _____, _____, _____   b) 75, 70, _____, _____, _____, _____

c) 36, 31, _____, _____, _____, _____   d) 54, 49, _____, _____, _____, _____

5. Start at 5. Skip count by 5s until 100.

5	10								
55	60								

6. Skip count by 25s from 0 by circling every fifth number in the chart

in Question 5. 0, _____, _____, _____, _____

7. Start at 25. Circle the numbers you say when skip counting by 25s.

25 30 35 40 45 50 55 60 65 70 75 80 85 90 95 100 105 110 115 120 125 130 135 140 145 150

Write the tens and ones digits of the numbers you circled. Continue the pattern.

_____ , _____ , _____ , _____ , _____ , _____ , _____ , _____ , _____ , _____

8. Complete the pattern by skip counting by 25s.

a) 50, 75, _____ , _____ , _____

b) 275, 300, _____ , _____ , _____

c) 125, 150, _____ , _____ , _____

d) 450, 475, _____ , _____ , _____

9. Skip count backwards by 25s to complete the pattern.

a) 125, 100, _____ , _____ , _____

b) 425, 400, _____ , _____ , _____

c) 875, 850, _____ , _____ , _____

d) 150, 125, _____ , _____ , _____

10. Write the pattern in the ones digits.

a) You start at 0 and skip count by 5 or 25. _____

b) You start at 0 and skip count by 10 or 100. _____

11. Fred counts by 25s starting at 25. He writes 25, 50, 75, 125, 150, 175, 200. Has he counted correctly? Explain.

_____

12. Skip count by 100s.

a) 100, 200, _____ , _____ , _____ , _____ , _____

b) What will be the ninth number in this list? _____

BONUS ▶ Skip count by 200s.

c) 200, 400, _____ , _____ , _____

d) 100, 300, _____ , _____ , _____

NS3-77 Counting Coins

penny
1 cent
1¢

nickel
5 cents
5¢

dime
10 cents
10¢

quarter
25 cents
25¢

loonie
100 cents
100¢

1. Fill in the blank.

a) _____ pennies make a nickel

b) _____ pennies make a dime

c) _____ nickels make a dime

d) _____ nickels make a quarter

e) _____ pennies make a loonie

f) _____ quarters make a loonie

2. Skip count by 5s starting from the given number.

a) 5, _____, _____, _____, _____

b) 40, _____, _____, _____, _____

3. Count on by nickels starting from the given amount.

a) 15, _____, _____, _____, _____

b) 65, _____, _____, _____, _____

4. Skip count by 10s starting from the given number.

a) 20, _____, _____, _____, _____

b) 60, _____, _____, _____, _____

5. Count on by dimes starting from the given amount.

a) 20, _____, _____, _____, _____

b) 15, _____, _____, _____, _____

6. Skip count by 25s starting from the given number.

a) 75, _____, _____, _____, _____

b) 25, _____, _____, _____, _____

7. Count on by quarters starting from the given amount.

a) 25, _____, _____, _____   b) 125, _____, _____, _____

c) 50, _____, _____, _____   d) 175, _____, _____, _____

8. Count on by 5s and then by 1s.

a) 5, __10__, _____ | __16__ , __17__ , _____ , _____
　　Count by 5s. | Continue counting by 1s.

b) 35, _____ | _____ , _____ , _____ , _____ , _____
　　Count by 5s. | Continue counting by 1s.

9. Count on by the first coin value given and then by the second coin value.

a) _____ , _____ , _____ , _____ | _____ , _____ , _____

b) _____ , _____ , _____ | _____ , _____ , _____ , _____

10. Count on by 10s and then by 5s.

a) 10, __20__ , _____ | __35__ , __40__ , _____ , _____
　　Count by 10s. | Continue counting by 5s.

b) 35, _____ | _____ , _____ , _____ , _____ , _____
　　Count by 10s. | Continue counting by 5s.

11. Count on by the first coin value given and then by the second coin value.

a) _____, _____, _____ | _____, _____, _____, _____

b) _____, _____, _____ | _____, _____, _____, _____

12. Circle the groups of coins that add up to a quarter.

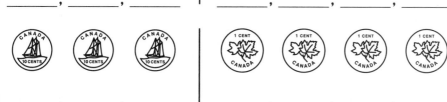

13. Count on by 25s and then by 5s.

a) 25, _____, _____ | _____, _____, _____, _____
   Count by 25s. | Continue counting by 5s.

b) 275, _____ | _____, _____, _____, _____, _____
   Count by 25s. | Continue counting by 5s.

14. Count on by the first coin value given and then by the second coin value.

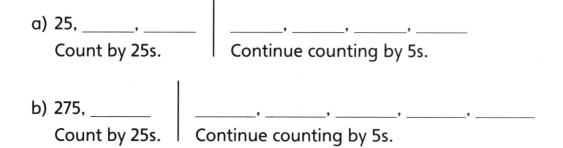

a) _____, _____, _____, _____, _____, _____

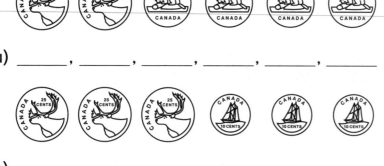

b) _____, _____, _____, _____, _____, _____

NS3-78 Counting On by Two or More Coin Values

I. Write the numbers in order from greatest to least.

a) 10, 25, 25, 5, I

__25__ , __25__ , __10__ , __5__ , __I__

b) 5, I, 10, 25, 10, 5

_____, _____, _____, _____, _____, _____

c) 5, 25, 10, I, 5

_____, _____, _____, _____, _____

d) 25, 10, 5, 25, I, 5

_____, _____, _____, _____, _____, _____

2. Write the value of the coins in order from greatest value to least value.

a) (10¢) (25¢) (I¢) (5¢)

(25¢) (10¢) (5¢) (I¢)

b) (10¢) (10¢) (5¢) (25¢)

( ) ( ) ( ) ( )

c) (5¢) (25¢) (10¢) (5¢)

( ) ( ) ( ) ( )

d) (I¢) (10¢) (25¢) (I¢)

( ) ( ) ( ) ( )

3. Count on to find the total.

a) __25__ , __50__ | __60__ , _____, _____ | _____, _____

Count by 25s. | Count by 10s. | Count by 5s.

b) __10__ , _____, _____ | _____, _____ | _____, _____

Count by 10s. | Count by 5s. | Count by Is.

c) __25__ , _____, _____ | _____, _____ | _____, _____

Count by 25s. | Count by 5s. | Count by Is.

d) __25__ , _____ | _____, _____ | _____, _____ | _____

Count by 25s. | Count by 10s. | Count by 5s. | Count by Is.

4. Count on by the first coin value given and then by the next coin value.

a) _____ , _____ , _____ , _____   b) _____ , _____ , _____ , _____ , _____

c) _____ , _____ , _____ , _____   d) _____ , _____ , _____ , _____ , _____

e) _____ , _____ , _____ , _____   f) _____ , _____ , _____ , _____ , _____

5. Write the value of the coins in order from greatest value to least value. Then count on to find the total amount.

a)   b)

   25¢ , 50¢ , 60¢ , 70¢   _____ , _____ , _____ , _____

c)   d)

_____ , _____ , _____ , _____   _____ , _____ , _____ , _____

e)   f)

_____ , _____ , _____ , _____   _____ , _____ , _____ , _____

6. What is the total amount in cents? Count on by the greatest coin value first.

a)

Total amount = _____

b)

Total amount = _____

c)

Total amount = _____

d)

Total amount = _____

e)

Total amount = _____

7. Write the name of the coin that has the same value as the given coins.

a)

_____

b)

_____

c)

_____

d)

_____

8. Estimate the total value of the coins in cents. Count the value to check your answer.

Coins		Estimate	Actual Value
a)			
b)			

9. Evan has 4 dimes, 3 quarters, and 2 nickels. How much money does he have?

Number Sense 3-78

NS3-79 What Coins Are Missing?

1. Fill in the missing amounts by counting on by 5s.

   a) 16, __21__, _____, 31   b) 30, _____, _____, 45   c) 45, _____, _____, 60

   d) 18, _____, _____, 33   e) 81, _____, _____, 96   f) 67, _____, _____, 82

2. Draw the extra nickels needed to make the total.

   a) 35¢

   (25¢) (5¢) (5¢)

   b) 16¢

   (10¢) (1¢)

   c) 25¢

   (10¢)

   d) 40¢

   (10¢) (10¢)

3. Fill in the missing amounts by counting on by 10s.

   a) 21, __31__, _____, 51   b) 49, _____, _____, 79   c) 45, _____, _____, 75

   d) _____, 47, _____, 67   e) _____, _____, 72, 82   f) _____, 35, _____, 55

4. Draw the extra dimes needed to make the total.

   a) 40¢

   (25¢) (5¢)

   b) 71¢

   (25¢) (25¢) (1¢)

   c) 90¢

   (25¢) (25¢)

   d) 55¢

   (10¢) (10¢) (5¢)

5. Sara has 2 quarters and 3 nickels. How many dimes does she need to make 85¢?

   _____

6. John has 3 quarters and 1 nickel. How many nickels does he need to make 95¢?

   _____

7. Fill in the missing amounts by counting on by 25s.

a) 25, _____, _____, 100

b) 75, _____, _____, 150

c) 125, _____, _____, 200

d) _____, 75, _____, 125

e) _____, 250, _____, 300

f) 3, 28, _____, _____

8. Draw the extra quarters needed to make the total.

a) 100¢

b) 125¢

25¢

c) 76¢

1¢

d) 105¢

5¢

9. Write the two coin values needed to make the total.

a) 65¢

25¢ 25¢ ◯ ◯

b) 135¢

c) 46¢

25¢ 10¢ ◯ ◯

d) 71¢

25¢ 25¢ 10¢ ◯ ◯

e) 140¢

100¢ 25¢ ◯ ◯

f) 195¢

100¢ 25¢ 25¢ 25¢ ◯ ◯

10. Write the value of the missing coins needed to make 185¢.

a) 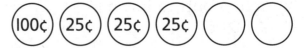 25¢ 100¢ 10¢ 25¢ 10¢ ◯ ◯

b) 25¢ 25¢ 25¢ 25¢ 25¢ 25¢ 25¢ ◯

11. Write the name of the missing coin needed to make the total.

a) 90¢

_____

b) 65¢

_____

c) 120¢

_____

d) 135¢

_____

e) 225¢

_____

f) 300¢

_____

12. Write the value of the missing coin needed to make the total.

a) Clara wants to buy a pen for 35¢.

    ◯

b) Ivan wants to buy a notebook for 235¢.

c) Sally wants to buy milk for 120¢.

d) Eddy wants to buy a snack for 75¢.

13. Ren has 1 dime, 3 quarters, 2 loonies, and 2 nickels. He wants to buy a key chain that costs 325¢. What coins is he missing?

_____

NS3-80 Least Number of Coins

1. Write the value of a single coin that has the same value as the given coins.

a) 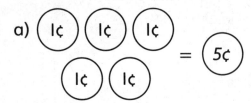 = 5¢

b)  = ◯

c) 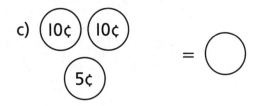 = ◯

d) 5¢ 5¢ 5¢ / 5¢ 5¢ = ◯

e) 10¢ 5¢ / 5¢ 5¢ = ◯

f) 25¢ 25¢ / 25¢ 25¢ = ◯

2. Fill in the blanks.

   a) 2 nickels have the same value as I _____.

   b) I quarter has the same value as _____ dimes and _____ nickel.

   c) I nickel has the same value as _____ pennies.

   d) _____ quarters have the same value as I _____.

   e) I quarter has the same value as _____ nickels.

   BONUS ▶ I loonie has the same value as _____ dimes.

3. Lily has 3 quarters, 2 dimes, and I nickel.

   a) What is the total value of her money? _____

   b) What single coin has the same value? _____

4. Raj has 7 dimes and 6 nickels.

   a) What is the total value of his money? _____

   b) What single coin has the same value? _____

5. Regroup coins to make the same total with the least number of coins.

a)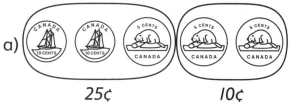

25¢   10¢

b)

c)

d)

e)

BONUS ▶

6. How much of the total amount could you pay in quarters? Draw the quarters to show your answer.

	Total Amount	Greatest Amount You Could Pay in Quarters
a)	60¢	(25¢) (25¢)
c)	45¢	

	Total Amount	Greatest Amount You Could Pay in Quarters
b)	80¢	
d)	95¢	

7. How much of the total amount could you pay in dimes? Draw the dimes to show your answer.

	Total Amount	Greatest Amount You Could Pay in Dimes
a)	25¢	(10¢) (10¢)
c)	42¢	

	Total Amount	Greatest Amount You Could Pay in Dimes
b)	15¢	
d)	37¢	

8. How much of the total amount could you pay in quarters? Show the amount left over by drawing the least number of coins.

	Total Amount	Amount You Could Pay in Quarters	Amount Remaining	Coins
a)	90¢	75¢	90¢ − 75¢ = 15¢	(10¢) (5¢)
b)	45¢			
c)	65¢			
d)	95¢			
e)	96¢			

9. Draw the least number of coins to make the total. Start by finding the greatest amount you can make in quarters.

a) 30¢ (10¢) (10¢) (10¢) incorrect
(25¢) (5¢) correct

b) 65¢

c) 70¢

d) 40¢

e) 95¢

f) 45¢

10. Draw the least number of coins to make the total. Start by finding the greatest amount you can make in loonies.

a) 105¢ (100¢) (5¢)

b) 125¢

c) 160¢

d) 175¢

e) 140¢

f) 190¢

NS3-81 Finding the Difference Using Mental Math

1. Calculate the difference owed for the purchase.

   a) Price of a pencil = 45¢

      Amount paid = 50¢

      Difference = __5¢__

   b) Price of an eraser = 25¢

      Amount paid = 30¢

      Difference = _____

   c) Price of a pen = 85¢

      Amount paid = 90¢

      Difference = _____

   d) Price of a ruler = 52¢

      Amount paid = 60¢

      Difference = _____

   e) Price of a marker = 74¢

      Amount paid = 80¢

      Difference = _____

   f) Price of a notebook = 66¢

      Amount paid = 70¢

      Difference = _____

2. Count on by 10s to find the difference owed from a dollar (100¢).

   a)

Price	Difference
80¢	20¢
70¢	
20¢	

   b)

Price	Difference
40¢	
60¢	
30¢	

   c)

Price	Difference
50¢	
10¢	
90¢	

3. Find the difference owed for the purchase. Count on by 10s.

   a) Price of a lollipop = 50¢

      Amount paid = 100¢

      Difference = _____

   b) Price of a mango = 80¢

      Amount paid = 100¢

      Difference = _____

   c) Price of an apple = 20¢

      Amount paid = 100¢

      Difference = _____

   d) Price of a banana = 60¢

      Amount paid = 100¢

      Difference = _____

4. Find the difference owed.

a) Price of a peach = 70¢

Amount paid = 100¢

Difference = _____

b) Price of a pencil = 30¢

Amount paid = 100¢

Difference = _____

c) Price of a gumball = 10¢

Amount paid = 100¢

Difference = _____

d) Price of a juice box = 40¢

Amount paid = 100¢

Difference = _____

You need to pay 15¢. You have a dollar (100¢). Find the difference owed.

Step 1: Find the smallest multiple of 10 greater than 15¢.

15¢ ⟶ 20¢ ⟶ 100¢

Step 2: Find the differences: 20 − 15 and 100 − 20.

15¢ —5→ 20¢ —80→ 100¢

Step 3: Add the differences: 5¢ + 80¢. Difference = 85¢

5. Find the difference owed from a dollar for the given amount.

a)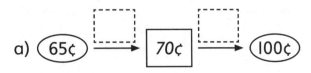

Difference = _____

b)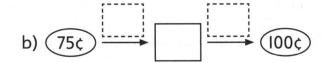

Difference = _____

c)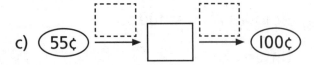

Difference = _____

d)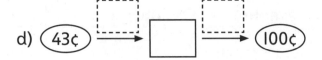

Difference = _____

6. Find the difference owed from a dollar for the given amount.

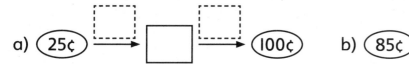

a) (25¢) ⤍ ☐ ⤍ (100¢)

Difference = _____

b) (85¢) ⤍ ☐ ⤍ (100¢)

Difference = _____

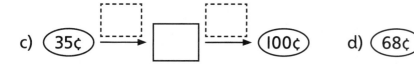

c) (35¢) ⤍ ☐ ⤍ (100¢)

Difference = _____

d) (68¢) ⤍ ☐ ⤍ (100¢)

Difference = _____

e) (57¢) ⤍ ☐ ⤍ (100¢)

Difference = _____

f) (62¢) ⤍ ☐ ⤍ (100¢)

Difference = _____

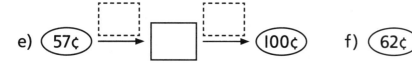

g) (47¢) ⤍ ☐ ⤍ (100¢)

Difference = _____

h) (79¢) ⤍ ☐ ⤍ (100¢)

Difference = _____

7. Find the difference owed from a dollar (100¢). Do the work in your head.

a) 85¢ _____   b) 65¢ _____   c) 25¢ _____   d) 45¢ _____

e) 35¢ _____   f) 95¢ _____   g) 55¢ _____   h) 70¢ _____

i) 75¢ _____   j) 13¢ _____   k) 29¢ _____   l) 41¢ _____

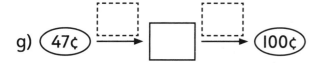

BONUS ▶ Find the difference owed in your head.

a) Price = 35¢

   Amount paid = 75¢

   Difference = _____

b) Price = 56¢

   Amount paid = 80¢

   Difference = _____

NS3-82 Counting Money with Dollars

one dollar = $1 = 100¢

 loonie
100¢
$1

 **toonie**
200¢
$2

 **5-dollar bill**
500¢
$5

1. Write the number of dollars using cents.

a) $4 = __400__ ¢   b) $3 = _____ ¢   c) $7 = _____ ¢

2. Write the number of cents using dollars.

a) 200¢ = $_2_   b) 600¢ = $____   c) 300¢ = $____

3. Fill in the blanks.

a) _____ loonies make a toonie

b) _____ loonies make a 5-dollar bill

c) _____ toonie and _____ loonies make a 5-dollar bill

d) _____ toonies and _____ loonie make a 5-dollar bill

We say the number of dollars and number of cents separately.

1 dollar and 35 cents
$1 and 35¢

2 dollars and 65 cents
$2 and 65¢

---

4. Draw the least number of coins to make the total.

a) $1 and 35¢   b) $2 and 90¢

c) $3 and 65¢   d) $4 and 70¢

5. Write the number of dollars and cents.

a)  $\_\_\_\_\_$ and $\_\_\_\_\_$ ¢

b)  $\_\_\_\_\_$ and $\_\_\_\_\_$ ¢

c) $\_\_\_\_\_$ and $\_\_\_\_\_$ ¢

d)  $\_\_\_\_\_$ and $\_\_\_\_\_$ ¢

e)  $\_\_\_\_\_$ and $\_\_\_\_\_$ ¢

6. Write the value of the missing coin needed to make the total.

a) $2 and 60¢

b) $3 and 40¢

c) $8 and 35¢

d) $7 and 40¢

7. Regroup coins to make the same total with the least number of coins or bills.

a)

$2 $1   25¢

b)

c)

BONUS ▶

8. Estimate to the nearest dollar. Then count the total starting with the highest coins first.

a)

Estimate $_____

Total $_____ and _____¢

b)

Estimate $_____

Total $_____ and _____¢

c)

Estimate $_____

Total $_____ and _____¢

9. Anna has 3 quarters, 2 loonies, 1 toonie, and a 5-dollar bill. She wants to buy lunch for her mom. It costs $12. How much more money does she need?

1. Count on to 100 by the first number.

    a) 10, 20, _____, _____, _____, _____, _____, _____, _____, _____

    b) 5, 10, _____, _____, _____, _____, _____, _____, _____, _____, _____,

    _____, _____, _____, _____, _____, _____, _____, _____, _____

    c) 25, _____, _____, _____

2. Use your answers to Question 1 to fill in the blank.

    a) _____ dimes in a loonie   b) _____ nickels in a loonie

    c) _____ quarters in a loonie   **BONUS ▶** _____ pennies in a loonie

3. Fill in the blanks to find the number of coins in a toonie.

    a) Dimes in a toonie

    ( ) = ( ) + ( ) = __10__ ( ) + __10__ ( ) = __20__ ( )

    b) Nickels in a toonie

    ( ) = ( ) + ( ) = _____ ( ) + _____ ( ) = _____ ( )

    c) Quarters in a toonie

    ( ) = ( ) + ( ) = _____ ( ) + _____ ( ) = _____ ( )

    d) Pennies in a toonie

    ( ) = ( ) + ( ) = _____ ( ) + _____ ( ) = _____ ( )

    BONUS ▶ Pennies in a toonie and a loonie

    ( ) ( ) = _____ ( ) + _____ ( ) = _____ ( )

4. Find different ways of adding to 5 using only the numbers 1 and 2.

a) 5 = __1__ + __1__ + __1__ + __1__ + __1__

b) 5 = ____ + ____ + ____

c) 5 = ____ + ____ + ____ + ____

5. Fill in the blanks to show different ways of making $5.

a)  = __5__

b)

c)

6. Find the total amount of money.

a)  $_____   b)  $_____

c)  $_____   d)  $_____

7. Count the dollars and cents separately.

a) $_____ and _____¢

b) $_____ and _____¢

c) $_____ and _____¢

8. Find the total number of dollars and cents.

	5 bill	2 DOLLARS	DOLLAR	25 CENTS	10 CENTS	5 CENTS	$	¢
a)	1	1	1	0	2	1	8	25
b)	1	0	1	3	0	1		
c)	0	2	1	1	2	1		
d)	1	1	0	3	2	0		

9. Tina needs $9 and 75¢ to buy a remote-controlled car. She has one 5-dollar bill, one toonie, and two quarters. What coins does she still need to buy the car? Use the least number of coins.

_____

10. Jake's lunch costs 7 dollars and 25 cents. He pays using two 5-dollar bills. The cashier gives him one toonie and two quarters back. Is that the correct difference? Explain.

_____

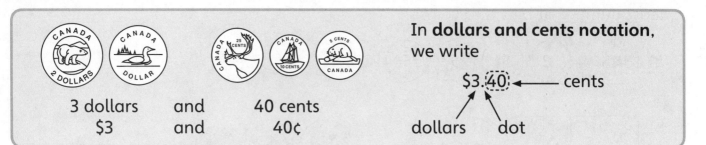

3 dollars   and   40 cents
$3   and   40¢

In **dollars and cents notation,** we write

$3.40 ⟵ cents

dollars   dot

1. Write the number of dollars and cents.

a) $7.25 $_____ and _____¢   b) $4.10 $_____ and _____¢

c) $3.47 $_____ and _____¢   d) $5.00 $_____ and _____¢

e) $10.75 $_____ and _____¢   f) $8.05 $_____ and _____¢

2. Write the value in dollars and cents notation.

a) 4 dollars and 25 cents   _$4.25_   b) 2 dollars and 80 cents   _____

c) $3 and 75¢   _____   d) $9 and 95¢   _____

e) $6 and 99¢   _____   **BONUS ▶** $7 and 5¢   _____

3. Find the total number of dollars and cents. Write the answer in dollars and cents notation.

a)  $_3_ and _60_ ¢

_$3.60_

b)  $_____ and _____¢

_____

c)   $_____ and _____¢

_____

d)  $_____ and _____¢

_____

4. Write the value of the money needed to make the total. Use the least number of bills and coins.

a) $3.75

b) $2.40

c) $6.90

d) $4.05

BONUS ▶

$8.95

5. a) Jay writes the value of the coins shown as $3.50.
Is he correct? Explain.

_____

_____

b) Yu thinks that $8.07 and $8.70 have the same value.
Is she correct? Explain.

_____

_____

6. Draw two more collections of coins that have a value of $4.75.

$4.75

$4.75

$4.75

10-dollar bill
$10

20-dollar bill
$20

50-dollar bill
$50

100-dollar bill
$100

I. Count on by 10s to 100.

____10____, _____, _____, _____, _____, _____, _____, _____, _____, _____

2. Find the number of $10 bills.

a) $20 = _____ $10 bills   b) $50 = _____ $10 bills   c) $100 = _____ $10 bills

3. Find the different ways of adding to 50 using only the numbers 10 and 20.

a) 50 = _____ + _____ + _____ + _____ + _____

b) 50 = _____ + _____ + _____

c) 50 = _____ + _____ + _____ + _____

4. Fill in the blanks to find different ways of making $50.

c) [50] = _____ [20] + _____ [10]

5. Find three ways of making $100 using $10 bills, $20 bills, or $50 bills.

6. Find the total amount of money.

a) $ _____

b) $ _____

c) $ _____

7. Lynn decides to save the money she received for her birthday. She has one $100 bill, three $50 bills, two $20 bills, and four $10 bills.

a) How much money does she have altogether? _____

b) Lynn wants to buy a tablet computer that costs $350.

How much more money does she need to save? _____

A **bank account** is a record of money you keep at a bank.

A **deposit** is money you put into a bank account.
A **withdrawal** is money you take out of a bank account.
The **balance** is the amount of money in the account.

---

8. The starting balance is $330. Find the balance after each operation.

Operation	Rough Work	Balance
Withdrawal: $20	330 − 20 = 310	$310
Deposit: $20	310 + _____ = _____	
Withdrawal: $35		
Deposit: $27		

9. Eric has a balance of $330 in his account. Find the amount of money Eric has in the bank after each operation.

a) Eric withdraws $40 from the bank and spends it on a jacket.

b) Eric earns $30 and deposits it into his bank account.

c) Does he have enough money to buy a pair of skis for $350? Explain.

10. Count the number of dollars and the number of cents. Write your answer in dollars and cents notation.

	$	¢	Answer
a)	13	40	$13.40
b)			
c)			
BONUS			

11. Write the value of the money needed to make the total. Use the least number of bills and coins.

a) $23.60 [$20] ($2) ($1) (25¢) (25¢) (10¢)

b) $37.40 [   ] [   ] [   ] ( ) ( ) ( ) ( )

c) $61.15 [   ] [   ] ( ) ( ) ( )

BONUS ▶ Find the total amount of money in dollars and cents notation.

_____

NS3-86 Multiplication and Money

> **REMINDER ▶** Multiplication is repeated addition.
>
> 4×5 3×10 2×25
>
> $= 5 + 5 + 5 + 5$ $= 10 + 10 + 10$ $= 25 + 25$
>
> $= 20$ $= 30$ $= 50$

1. Multiply by using repeated addition.

   a) 4×10

      = _____

      = _____

   b) 3×25

      = _____

      = _____

   c) 6×5

      = _____

      = _____

   d) 3×20

      = _____

      = _____

   e) 3×50

      = _____

      = _____

   f) 2×100

      = _____

      = _____

> **REMINDER ▶** You can multiply by skip counting.
>
> 4×5 3×10 2×25
>
> 5, 10, 15, ⟨20⟩   10, 20, ⟨30⟩   25, ⟨50⟩

2. Multiply by skip counting. Circle the answer.

   a) 4×10

      _10, 20, 30, ⟨40⟩_

   b) 4×25

      _____

   c) 6×5

      _____

   d) 5×20

      _____

   e) 2×50

      _____

   f) 3×100

      _____

   g) 3×5

      _____

   h) 2×10

      _____

   i) 4×20

      _____

   j) 3×25

      _____

   k) 7×5

      _____

   l) 5×10

      _____

3. Write a multiplication equation to find the total value of the coins.

a) 4 nickels

$4 \times 5¢ = 20¢$

b) 5 dimes

_____

c) 2 quarters

_____

d) 3 quarters

_____

e) 2 nickels

_____

f) 6 dimes

_____

You can use multiplication and addition when you have more than one type of coin.

4 nickels and 3 dimes

$(4 \times 5¢) + (3 \times 10¢)$

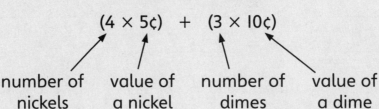

number of nickels · value of a nickel · number of dimes · value of a dime

4. Use multiplication and addition to write the value of the coins.

a) 2 nickels and 3 dimes

_____

b) 4 nickels and 2 dimes

_____

c) 2 quarters and 3 nickels

_____

5. Use multiplication and addition to write the value of the coins.
Then find the total value.

a)

$(2 \times 25¢) + (3 \times 10¢)$

$= 50¢ + 30¢$

$= 80¢$

b)

_____

$=$ _____

$=$ _____

c)

_____

$=$ _____

$=$ _____

d)

_____

$=$ _____

$=$ _____

6. Write a multiplication equation to find the total value of the bills and coins.

a) three toonies

$\underline{\quad 3 \times \$2 = \$6 \quad}$

b) four 10-dollar bills

$\underline{\hspace{3cm}}$

c) three 5-dollar bills

$\underline{\hspace{3cm}}$

d) four loonies

$\underline{\hspace{3cm}}$

e) two 5-dollar bills

$\underline{\hspace{3cm}}$

BONUS ▶ five 20-dollar bills

$\underline{\hspace{3cm}}$

7. Use multiplication and addition to write the value of the bills and coins.

a) two toonies and three loonies

$\underline{\quad (2 \times \$2) + (3 \times \$1) \quad}$

b) three loonies and two toonies

$\underline{\hspace{3cm}}$

c) two 5-dollar bills and three loonies

$\underline{\hspace{3cm}}$

BONUS ▶ two 50-dollar bills and three 10-dollar bills

$\underline{\hspace{3cm}}$

8. Use multiplication and addition to write the value of the bills and coins. Then find the total value.

a)

$\underline{\hspace{3cm}}$

$\underline{\hspace{3cm}}$

$\underline{\hspace{3cm}}$

b)

$\underline{\hspace{3cm}}$

$\underline{\hspace{3cm}}$

$\underline{\hspace{3cm}}$

9. Ethan wants to buy a birthday gift that costs $120. He has two 50-dollar bills and three 5-dollar bills. Does he have enough money? Explain.

$\underline{\hspace{8cm}}$

$\underline{\hspace{8cm}}$

You can make a deposit or withdraw money from your bank account using:

Cash	**Cheque**	**Bank Card**

1. Zack's mother has $750 in her bank account. She withdraws $120 to spend during the holidays. How much is left in her account? _____

2. Anne's parents have $940 in their shared bank account. Her mom wrote a cheque for $50 to pay for groceries. How much money is left in their account?

   _____

3. It is a good idea to keep track of the activity in your bank account. Find the balance left in the account after each operation.

Date	Deposit	Withdrawal	Balance
June 10			$350
June 18	$30		$380
July 3		$100	$280
July 6	$60		
August 2	$70		
August 8		$150	

4. A **credit card** lets you borrow money to pay for purchases. If you don't pay the credit card company the money owed at the end of the month, they will charge you extra.

   a) In June, Kate's older brother used his credit card to make purchases of $125, $50, $75, and $250. How much does he owe at the end of June?

   b) Kate's brother did not pay back the money to the credit card company in time. They charged him $50 extra. How much money does he need to pay back altogether?

Some ways students can earn money:

delivering newspapers

mowing lawns

running a lemonade stand

raking leaves

5. Ben has $250 in his bank account. Ben earns $5 each time he rakes leaves for one of his neighbours.

   a) Ben raked leaves on Thursday, Friday, Saturday, and Sunday.

     How much cash did he earn? _____

   b) Ben deposited all the cash into his bank account.

     How much money does he have in his bank account? _____

6. Kim sells lemonade for $2 a glass. She sold 30 glasses of lemonade yesterday.

   a) How much money did Kim collect? _____

   b) She paid $20 for the lemons. How much money did she earn?

   _____

7. At the start of summer, Nina has $300 in her bank account. She earns $10 each time she mows her neighbour's lawn. She is paid by cheque at the end of the summer.

   a) Nina mows her neighbour's lawn 20 times during the summer. What is the amount on the cheque she is given at the end of summer?

   _____

   b) Nina deposits the cheque into her bank account.

     How much is in her bank account at the end of the summer? _____

8. Anton earns 5¢ for each newspaper he delivers. Last week, Anton delivered 100 newspapers. How much money did he earn in dollars?

9. Emma has $500 in her bank account. She gets an allowance of $30 each month, but spends $25 of the allowance every month. How much will she have in her bank account after 3 months?

1. Count on by 5s to label the number line.

   a)
   0   5   10   50

   b)
   50   55   60   100

2. Write the multiple of 5 before the given number.

   a) 32 __30__   b) 47 __45__   c) 71 _____

   d) 18 _____   e) 93 _____   f) 28 _____

3. Write the multiple of 5 after the given number.

   a) 32 __35__   b) 47 __50__   c) 71 _____

   d) 18 _____   e) 93 _____   f) 28 _____

4. Write the multiples of 5 before and after the given number.

   a) 32 is between __30__ and __35__   b) 27 is between __25__ and _____

   c) 41 is between _____ and _____   d) 78 is between _____ and _____

   e) 56 is between _____ and _____   f) 18 is between _____ and _____

5. Circle the multiple of 5 that is closer to the number.

   a) 43   b) 21
      40   (45)   (20)   25

   c) 72   d) 89
      70   75   85   90

   e) 11   f) 98
      10   15   95   100

   g) 36   h) 62
      35   40   60   65

You can round 37 to the nearest multiple of 5.

Step 1: Find the multiple of 5 before 37.   35

Step 2: Find the multiple of 5 after 37.   40

Step 3: Choose the multiple of 5 closer to 37.

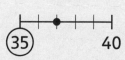

6. Complete the table to round the number to the nearest multiple of 5.

Number	Multiple of 5 Before	Multiple of 5 After	Picture	Nearest Multiple of 5
48	45	50	45 ⋯ 50	50
71				
34				
67				
22				
94				
13				

7. Round the money to the nearest nickel by rounding the number of cents to the nearest multiple of 5.

a) 81¢ _____   b) 39¢ _____   c) 14¢ _____

d) 41¢ _____   e) 26¢ _____   f) 68¢ _____

8. Lewis thinks that 73¢ rounded to the nearest nickel is 70¢. Is he correct? Explain.

_____

NS3-89 Giving Change (Advanced)

1. You have $10. Find the difference owed when you need to pay the given amount.

Amount to Pay	Paid	Calculation	Difference Owed
$2	$10	$10 − $2	$8
$4	$10		
$7	$10		
$3	$10		
$6	$10		

2. You have $1. Find the difference owed when you need to pay the given amount.

Amount to Pay	Paid	Calculation	Difference Owed
70¢	$1	100¢ − 70¢	30¢
40¢	$1		
60¢	$1		
90¢	$1		
50¢	$1		

3. Find the difference to the next highest dollar.

a) $2.30 ⟶ [70¢] $3.00

b) $5.80 ⟶ [ ] $6.00

c) $4.60 ⟶ [ ] _____

d) $1.90 ⟶ [ ] _____

e) $7.10 ⟶ [ ] _____

f) $0.20 ⟶ [ ] _____

g) $6.40 ⟶ [ ] _____

h) $7.80 ⟶ [ ] _____

You need to pay $6.40. You pay with a 10-dollar bill ($10.00). What is the difference owed?

Step 1: Find the next highest whole dollar after $6. $7

Step 2: Write the amount of money given. $10

Step 3: Find the differences in the steps.   60¢, $3

Step 4: Add the differences. $3.60

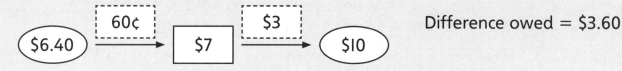

Difference owed = $3.60

4. You need to pay the given amount. You have a 10-dollar bill.
   Find the difference owed.

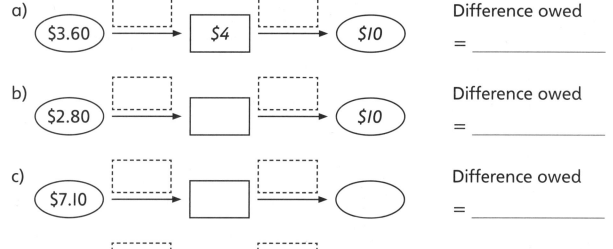

a) $3.60 → [ ] → $4 → [ ] → $10   Difference owed = _____

b) $2.80 → [ ] → [ ] → [ ] → $10   Difference owed = _____

c) $7.10 → [ ] → [ ] → [ ] → ( )   Difference owed = _____

d) $0.80 → [ ] → [ ] → [ ] → ( )   Difference owed = _____

BONUS ▶ You need to pay the given amount. You have a 20-dollar bill.
Find the difference owed.

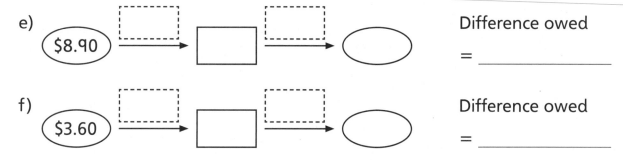

e) $8.90 → [ ] → [ ] → [ ] → ( )   Difference owed = _____

f) $3.60 → [ ] → [ ] → [ ] → ( )   Difference owed = _____

5. You need to pay the given amount. You have a 10-dollar bill.
Find the difference owed.

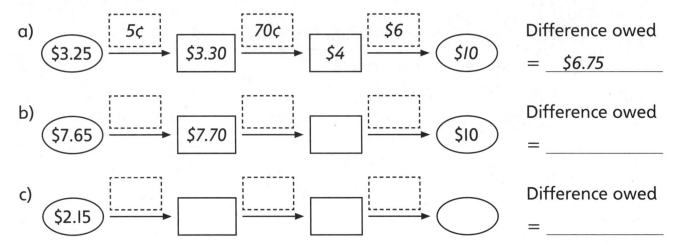

a) ($3.25) —5¢→ [$3.30] —70¢→ [$4] —$6→ ($10)   Difference owed
= __$6.75__

b) ($7.65) —[ ]→ [$7.70] —[ ]→ [ ] —[ ]→ ($10)   Difference owed
= _____

c) ($2.15) —[ ]→ [ ] —[ ]→ [ ] —[ ]→ ( )   Difference owed
= _____

6. Round the given amount to the nearest nickel by rounding the number
of cents to the nearest multiple of 5.

Money	$	¢	Cents Rounded to the Nearest Nickel	Money Rounded to the Nearest Nickel
$8.43	$8	43¢	45¢	$8.45
$2.21				
$9.78				
$3.07				

7. You need to pay the amount shown. You have a 10-dollar bill.
Round the amount to the nearest nickel. Then find the difference owed.

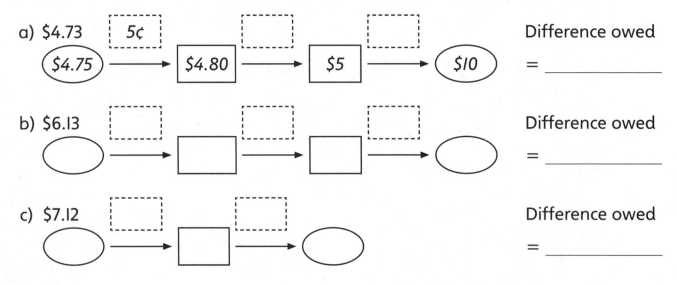

a) $4.73   [5¢] [ ] [ ]
($4.75) —→ [$4.80] —→ [$5] —→ ($10)   Difference owed
= _____

b) $6.13   [ ] [ ] [ ]
( ) —→ [ ] —→ [ ] —→ ( )   Difference owed
= _____

c) $7.12   [ ] [ ]
( ) —→ [ ] —→ ( )   Difference owed
= _____

G3-15 Translations

1. Count the squares to say how many units right the dot slides from A to B.

a)

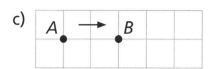

___3___ units right

b)

_____ units right

c)

_____ units right

2. Count the squares to say how many units left the dot slides from A to B.

a)

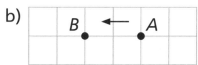

___5___ units left

b)

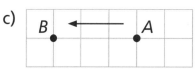

_____ units left

c)

_____ units left

3. Slide the dot.

a) 4 units right

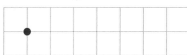

b) 6 units left

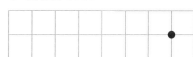

c) 7 units right

4. How many units right and how many units down does the dot slide from A to B?

a)

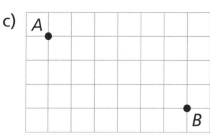

___4___ units right

___2___ units down

b)

_____ units right

_____ units down

c)

_____ units right

_____ units down

d)

_____ units right

_____ unit down

e)

_____ units right

_____ units down

f)

_____ units right

_____ units down

5. Slide the dot.

a) 4 units right, 2 units up b) 5 units left, 3 units up c) 3 units left, 3 units down

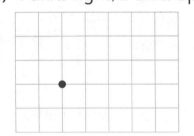 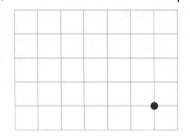 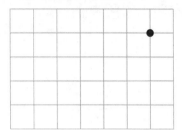

d) 2 units right, I unit down e) I unit left, 2 units down f) 5 units right, 2 units up

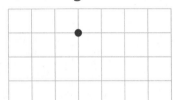 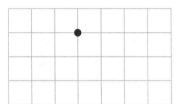 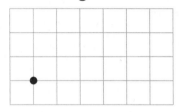

6. Shade the same shape on the second grid. Make sure the dots are on the same vertex of both shapes.

a)   b)   c)

d)   e)   f)

g) 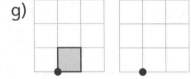 h) 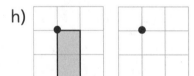 i)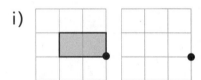

7. Copy the shape so that the dots are on the same vertex of both shapes.

a) 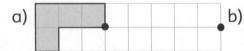 b)  c)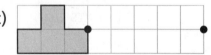

> When you slide a shape without turning or flipping it over, you **translate** it.

8. Translate the shape 5 units left. First slide the dot, then copy the shape.

a) 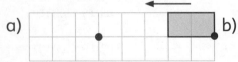 b) 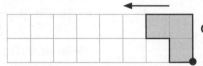 c)

Geometry 3-15

9. Translate the shape. First, draw the arrow to show the direction.
Slide the dot, then copy the shape.

a) 3 units right

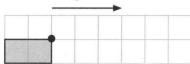

b) 3 units left

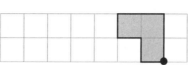

c) 4 units right

d) 2 units down

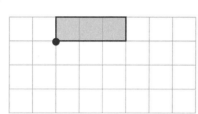

e) 2 units up

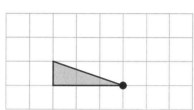

f) 3 units down

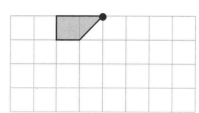

To translate a shape 5 units right and 2 units down:

Step 1: Draw a dot on any vertex of the shape.

Step 2: Draw an arrow the number of units right.

Step 3: Draw an arrow the number of units down from the end of the first arrow. Draw a dot at the end of the arrow.

Step 4: Draw the new shape so that the dots are on the same vertex of both shapes.

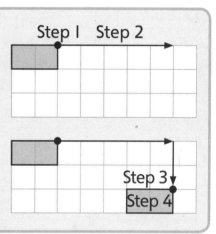

10. Do steps 1, 2, and 3 to translate the shape.

a) 3 units right, 1 unit up

b) 4 units left, 2 units down

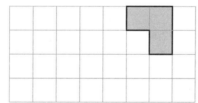

c) 3 units left, 2 units up

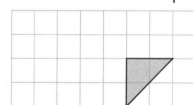

11. Translate the shape.

a) 3 units right, 2 units up

b) 1 unit left, 3 units up

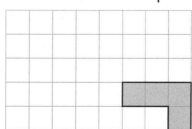

c) 5 units right, 1 unit down

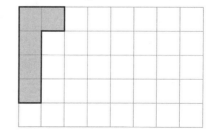

G3-16 Translations on Maps

To describe a translation of a dot, draw an arrow right or left, and another arrow up or down. Write the length of each arrow and the direction.

Example: To translate A to B, move A 3 units left and 2 units up.

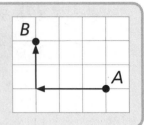

1. How many units right or left, and up or down, do you need to slide the star to get to the dot?

   A: _____ units up   B: _____ units right

   C: _____ units left, _____ unit down

   D: _____ units _____, _____ units up

   E: _____ units right, _____ units _____

   F: _____ unit _____, _____ units _____

   G: _____

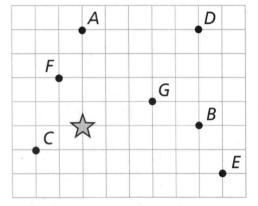

2. The dots on the map show Cathy's path through a swamp. The grey regions are bogs. Describe Cathy's path.

   a) From A to B __2 units right_____

   b) From B to C _____

   c) From C to D _____

   d) From D to E _____

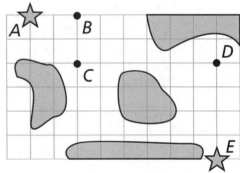

3. a) Describe the canoe path from A to F.

   From A to B _____

   From B to C _____

   From C to D _____

   From D to E _____

   From E to F _____

   b) Describe a shorter route from A to F.

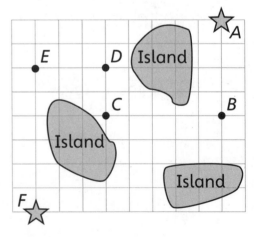

_____

4. a) Describe the path.

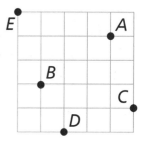

From A to B   _3 units left, 2 units down_

From D to C _____ units right, _____ unit up

From B to C _____

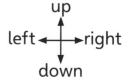

b) Underline the word "from." Circle the letter you need to start at.

Move <u>from</u> (A) to B.   Move to B from C.

Go to D from B.   Slide from D to A.

BONUS ▶ Go from A to D through B.

c) How can you get from B to D? _____

How can you get to A from C? _____

d) Marko moves 4 units right and 1 unit down from E.

Which point does he end at? _____

e) Which point is 2 units left and 5 units up from D? _____

f) Which point is 1 unit right and 3 units down from E? _____

5. Use the map and the direction arrows to answer the questions.

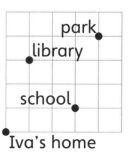

a) What place is 1 block east and 3 blocks north of Iva's home?

_____

b) What place is 2 blocks west and 2 blocks north of the school?

_____

c) What place is 1 block south and 3 blocks west of the school?

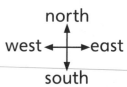

_____

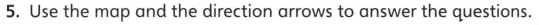

d) Describe how to get from the park to the school.

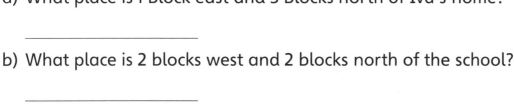

_____

e) Describe how to go to the library from the school.

_____

f) Describe how to go to the park from the library.

_____

Ben wants to get from square A to square B. He draws a dot on the same corner of both squares.

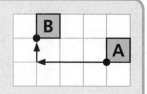

Ben describes how to translate the dot: 3 units left, I unit up. To get from A to B, go 3 units left and I unit up.

6. Describe how to translate square A to square B.

a)

_____ units _____

b)

_____ units _____

c)

_____ units _____,

_____ unit _____

BONUS ▶ The map below shows where students sit. Use the clues to fill in the missing names.

Mandy		Tristan	
	Kim		Amir
Avril		Tom	

a) Walk 2 desks down and I desk right from Tristan to find Jin's seat.

b) Lela's desk is I desk left of Amir.

c) Sally sits between Mandy and Tristan.

d) Walk 2 desks left and I desk up from Tom to find Zack's desk.

e) Tasha is I desk right of Tristan.

f) Fred sits between Avril and Tom.

7. Use the map to answer the questions.

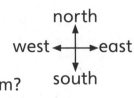

a) Eric travels 2 km east and I km north from the farm. Where does he go?

b) What is 2 kilometres north of the farm?

c) Tina is at the lake. Describe her path to the city.

d) How can you get to the hill from the lake?

BONUS ▶ Matt wants to get from the farm to the lake. He does not want to go over the hill. Describe his path.

G3-I7 Reflections

> **REMINDER** ▶ When you fold a shape and the parts match exactly, the fold is a
> line of symmetry.
>
> line of symmetry   not a line of symmetry   When you fold along
> the line, the top part
> does not cover the
> bottom part.

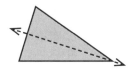 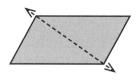 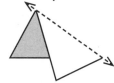

1. Draw the line of symmetry.

a)   b)   c)

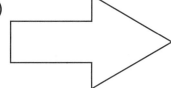  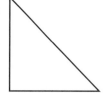

2. Does the shape have a line of symmetry? Write "yes" or "no."

a)   b)   c)

_____   _____   _____

> A line of symmetry is also called a **mirror line**. The halves of the shape are
> **mirror images** of each other. You can get one of them by flipping the other
> over the mirror line.

3. The dashed line is the mirror line. Finish drawing the mirror image.

a)   b)   c)

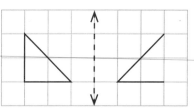 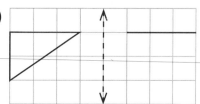 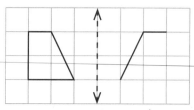

d)   e)   f)

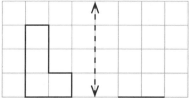 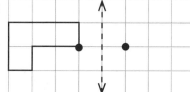 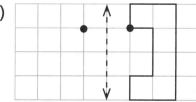

When you draw a mirror image of a shape, you **reflect** the shape in the mirror line.

4. Reflect the shape in the dashed mirror line.

a)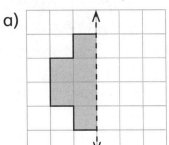

b)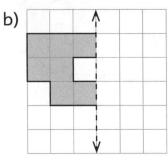

c)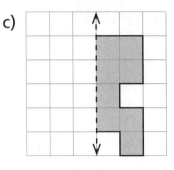

d)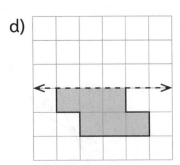

e)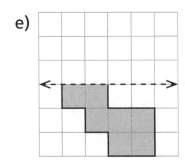

f)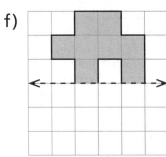

5. a) Draw your own shape on one side of the mirror line. Reflect it in the mirror line.

b) Are the shapes you drew congruent? How do you know?

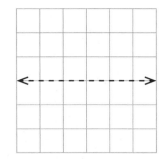

_____

_____

6. Grace makes a pattern by reflecting shapes in vertical lines. Draw the next 3 terms in her pattern.

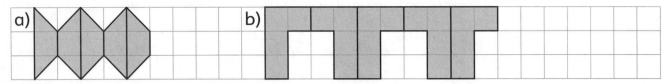

7. Use reflections to draw your own pattern of shapes.

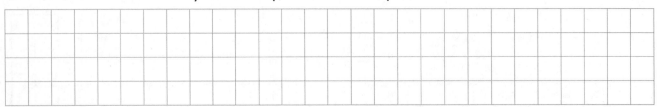

G3-18 Flips, Slides, and Turns

> When you turn a shape around a point without flipping it, you **rotate** it.

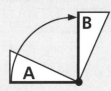 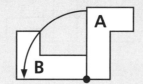 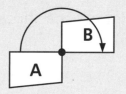

1. Was shape C rotated around a point to get shape D? Write "yes" or "no."

a)

b)

c)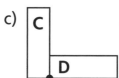

d)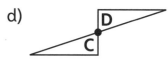

_____ _____ _____ _____

e)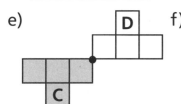

f)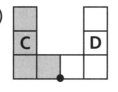

g)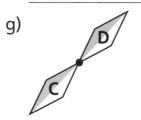

h)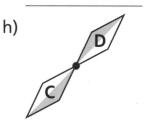

_____ _____ _____ _____

2. Which card, B, C, or D, is a rotation of card A? _____

A.

B.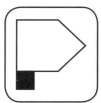

C.

D.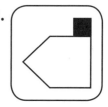

3. Which cards are a rotation of card E? _____

E.

F.

G.

H.

4. Ed makes a pattern by rotating a card with a smiley face. Draw the next 3 figures in his pattern. Hint: Describe the pattern using directions.

a) ☺ ☺ ☺ ☺ ☐ ☐ ☐

b) ☺ ☺ ☺ ☺ ☺ ☺ ☐ ☐ ☐

5. Do you need a translation or a reflection to get from one shape to the other? Circle the answer.

a)

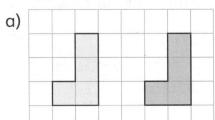

translation   reflection

b)

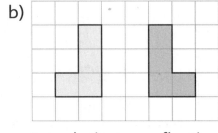

translation   reflection

c)

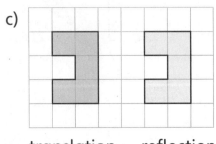

translation   reflection

d)

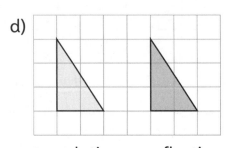

translation   reflection

e)

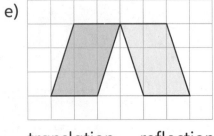

translation   reflection

f)

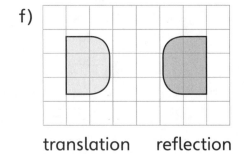

translation   reflection

g)

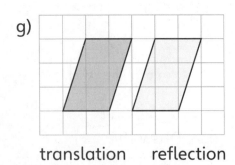

translation   reflection

h)

translation   reflection

6. Which attribute changes in a reflection: size, shape, or direction? _____

7. Do you need a translation, reflection, or rotation to get from one shape to the other? Choose one.

a)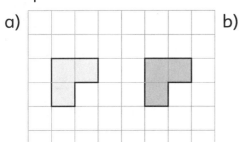

____translation____

b)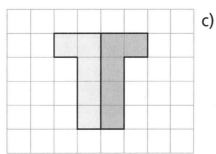

_____

c)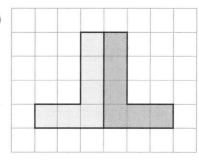

_____

d)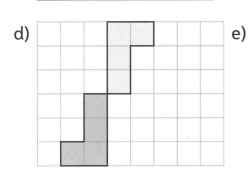

_____

e)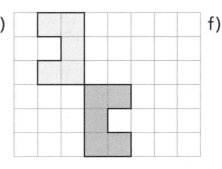

_____

f)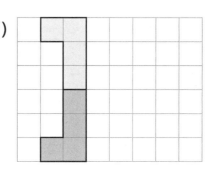

_____

g)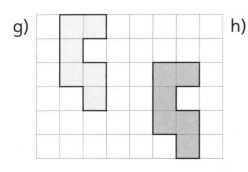

_____

h)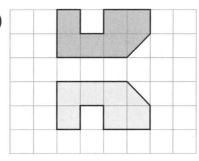

_____

i)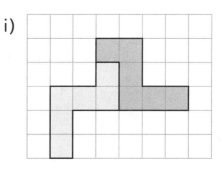

_____

BONUS ▶ List two different ways to get from one shape to the other.

a)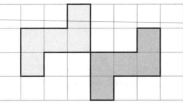

_____

_____

b)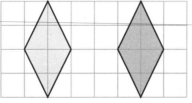

_____

_____

c)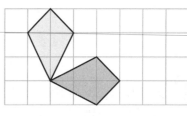

_____

_____

8. Kathy has two identical clear plastic cards. She reflects or rotates one of the cards and places it beside the other card. Did she reflect or rotate the card?

a)

rotate

b)

c)

d)

e)

f)

g)

h)

i)

9. One shape is reflected, rotated, or translated to make the pattern. Draw the next two shapes in the pattern. How was the pattern made?

a)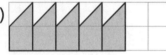

b)

c)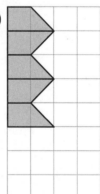

d)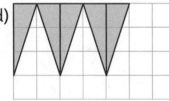

BONUS ▶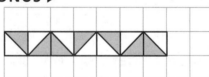

10. Jack makes a pattern using translations, reflections, and rotations. How did he get each new figure from the previous one?

Figure 1   Figure 2   Figure 3   Figure 4   Figure 5   Figure 6   Figure 7

Geometry 3-18

G3-19 3-D Shapes

Geometric shapes that are not flat are called **3-D shapes**.

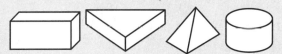
3-D shapes

flat shapes

1. Circle the 3-D shapes.

3-D shapes have **faces**, **edges**, and **vertices**.

Faces are flat. They meet at edges. Edges meet at vertices.

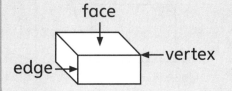

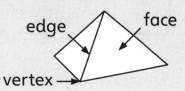

2. What is the shape of the shaded face?

a)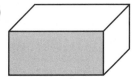

b)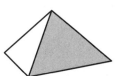

c)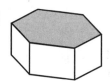

_____   _____   _____

3. Draw a dot on each vertex you see.

a)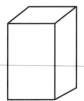

b)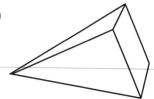

c)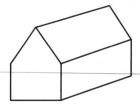

4. Trace the edges you see.

a)

b)

c)

You cannot see the edges on the back of the shape. Use dashed lines to show **hidden edges**.

hidden edges

5. The dot shows the hidden vertex. Draw dashed lines to show the hidden edges.

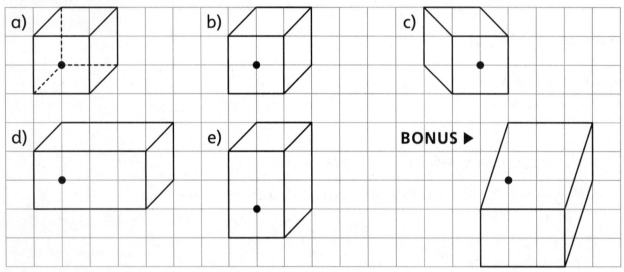

a)   b)   c)

d)   e)   BONUS ▶

6. How are the shapes in Question 5 different from each other? _____

_____

7. Count the edges.

a)

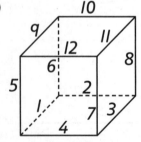

____12____ edges

b)

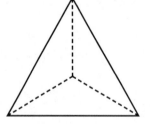

_____ edges

c)

_____ edges

d)

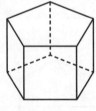

_____ edges

e)

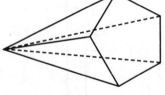

_____ edges

f)

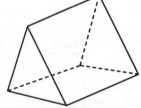

_____ edges

Geometry 3-19

8. Draw a dot on each vertex. Count the vertices.

a)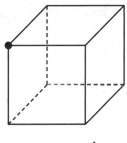

_____ vertices

b)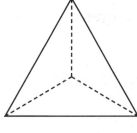

_____ vertices

c)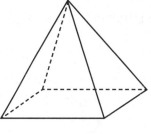

_____ vertices

9. a) Count the vertices and the edges.

A.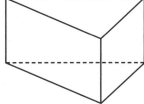

_____ vertices

_____ edges

B.

_____ vertices

_____ edges

C.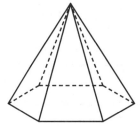

_____ vertices

_____ edges

D.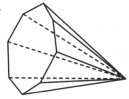

_____ vertices

_____ edges

E.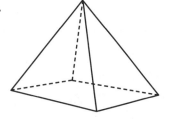

_____ vertices

_____ edges

F.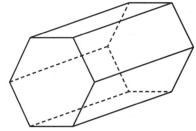

_____ vertices

_____ edges

b) Sort the shapes into the table and fill in the Venn diagram. Remember to put shapes with both properties into the central region.

7 or Fewer Vertices	10 or More Edges

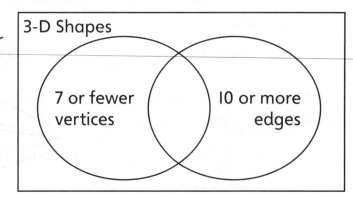

3-D Shapes

7 or fewer vertices

10 or more edges

G3-20 Building Pyramids and Prisms

A **skeleton** of a 3-D shape has only edges and vertices.

To make a skeleton of a **pyramid**:

Step 1: Make a polygon using clay balls for vertices and toothpicks for edges. The polygon is the **base** of the pyramid.

Step 2: Add a toothpick to each vertex.

Step 3: Join the loose toothpicks to one vertex at the top.

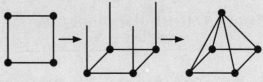

1. a) Make a pyramid using clay balls and toothpicks. Start with the given polygon. Fill in the table for each pyramid.

Starting Polygon (Base)	Triangle	Square	Pentagon	Hexagon
Number of Sides in the Base				
Number of Vertices in the Pyramid				
Number of Edges in the Pyramid				

b) Describe the pattern in the number of vertices in the pyramids.

_____

c) Describe the pattern in the number of edges in the pyramids.

_____

2. a) Fill in the table without making the pyramids. Extend the patterns from Question 1.

Number of Sides in the Base	7	8	9	10
Number of Vertices in the Pyramid				
Number of Edges in the Pyramid				

b) How can you get the number of vertices in the pyramid from the number of sides in the base? _____

c) The base of a pyramid has 20 sides. How many vertices does the pyramid have? _____

BONUS ▶ How many edges does the pyramid from part c) have? _____

To make a skeleton of a **prism**:

Step 1: Make two copies of the same polygon using clay balls for vertices and toothpicks for edges. They are the bases of the prism.

Step 2: Add a toothpick to each vertex of one of the bases.

Step 3: Attach the other base on top of the toothpicks.

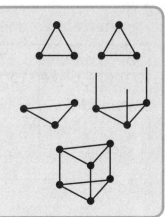

3. a) Make a prism using clay balls and toothpicks. Start with the given polygon. Fill in the table for each prism.

Shape of Base	Triangle	Square	Pentagon	Hexagon
Number of Vertices in the Prism				
Number of Edges in the Prism				

b) Describe the pattern in the number of vertices in the prisms.

_____

c) Describe the pattern in the number of edges in the prisms.

_____

4. a) Fill in the table without making the prisms.

Number of Sides in a Base	7	8	9	10
Number of Vertices in the Prism				
Number of Edges in the Prism				

b) How can you get the number of vertices in the prism from the number of sides in a base? _____

BONUS ▶ How can you get the number of edges in the prism from the number of sides in a base? _____

c) One base of a prism has 100 sides.

How many vertices does the prism have? _____

BONUS ▶ How many edges does the prism from part c) have? _____

Pyramids have one base. Use the shape of the base to name the pyramid.

Shape of Base	Triangle	Square	Rectangle	Pentagon
Name of Pyramid	triangular or triangle-based	square or square-based	rectangular or rectangle-based	pentagonal or pentagon-based
Pyramid				

5. a) The base of a pyramid is a hexagon. Name the pyramid.

_____

b) What is the shape of the base of an octagonal pyramid? _____

6. The base is shaded. Name the pyramid.

a)

b)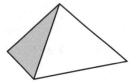

c)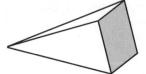

hexagonal pyramid   _____   _____

_____   _____   _____

Prisms have two bases. Use the shape of the base to name the prism.

Shape of Base	Triangle	Square	Rectangle	Pentagon
Name of Prism	triangular or triangle-based	square or square-based	rectangular or rectangle-based	pentagonal or pentagon-based
Prism				

7. One base is shaded. Name the prism.

a)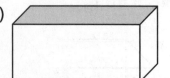

b)

c)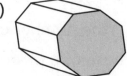

8. Dory thinks that the number of vertices in a prism is double the number of vertices in a base of the prism. Is she correct? Explain.

G3-21 Faces of 3-D Shapes

In pictures of 3-D shapes, faces that are rectangles or squares are not drawn as rectangles or squares with right angles. All faces of a **cube** are squares.

1. What is the shape of the shaded face?

a)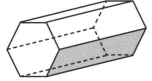

_____rectangle_____

b)

_____

c)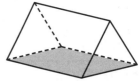

_____

d)

_____

e)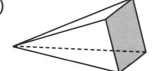

_____

f)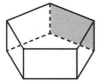

_____

2. Shade the face or faces of the given shape.

a) pentagon

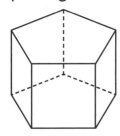

b) hexagon

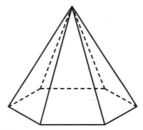

c) pentagon

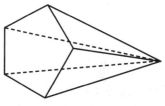

3. Count the faces.

a)

_____ faces

b)

_____ faces

c)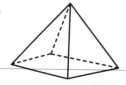

_____ faces

d)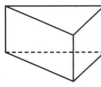

_____ faces

e)

_____ faces

f)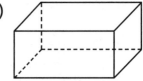

_____ faces

4. Use the shapes below to fill in the table and the Venn diagram.

A. 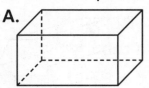   B.   C.   D.   E.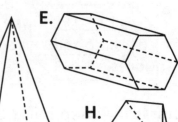

F.   G.   H.

Property	Shapes with the Property
5 faces or fewer	
6 faces	
7 faces or more	

3-D Shapes

6 or Fewer Faces   6 or More Faces

REMINDER ▶ Pyramids have one base and one vertex opposite it. Prisms have two identical bases.

pyramids   prisms

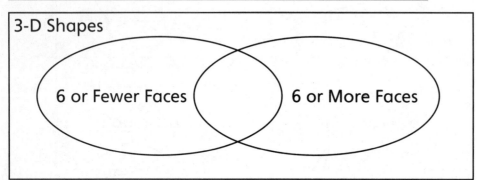

5. Shade the base or bases.

a) 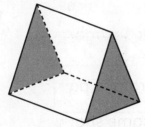   b) 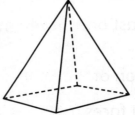   c) 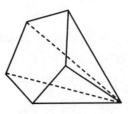   d)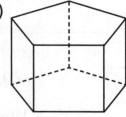

6. a) Use the shapes below to fill in the table and the Venn diagram.

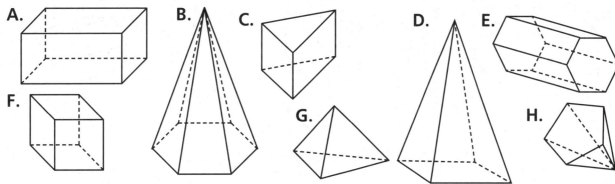

Property	Shapes with the Property
At least one face is a rectangle.	
At least one face is a triangle.	

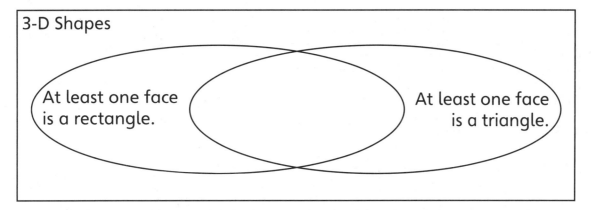

b) Circle the pyramids above in red. Circle them in the Venn diagram.

All pyramids have some faces that are _____.

c) Circle all the prisms above in blue. Circle them in the Venn diagram.

All prisms have some faces that are _____.

REMINDER ▶ Use the shape of the base to name the pyramid or the prism.

pentagonal pyramid   pentagonal prism

d) Two different 3-D shapes have at least one face that is a hexagon. Write the names of the shapes.

e) Name the shapes in the central region of the Venn diagram in part b).

BONUS ▶ Which shapes can have all faces that are the same shape and same size?

G3-22 Matching 3-D Shapes

You can cut and fold a **net** to make a 3-D shape. Example: net of a cube

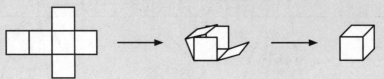

I. Match the net to the 3-D shape.

A. 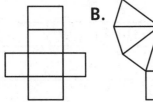 **B.**  **C.**   **D.**  **E.** 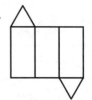 **F.**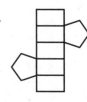

a)   b)   c)   d)   e)   f)

_____   _____   _____   _____   _____   _____

2. Match the shape to the name.

G.   **H.**   **I.**   **J.**   **K.**   **L.**   **M.**   **N.**

a) triangular pyramid _____   b) hexagonal prism _____

c) pentagonal pyramid _____   d) hexagonal pyramid _____

e) triangular prism _____   f) cube _____

g) rectangular prism _____   h) pentagonal prism _____

3. What 3-D shape am I?

a) I have 6 faces that are triangles and I face that is a hexagon.

_____

b) I have 6 faces that are rectangles and 2 faces that are hexagons.

_____

BONUS ▶ I have 10 faces in total. Only 8 of them are rectangles.

_____

4. a) Make the shape using a net. Then fill in the table.

| Shape | Name | Number of | | | Sketch of the Faces |
		Faces	Vertices	Edges	
	square pyramid	5	5	8	

b) Which two shapes have the same number of faces, vertices, and edges? How are these shapes the same and how are they different?

c) Which shapes have 6 vertices?

d) Which shape has 6 vertices and 5 faces?

e) Which shapes have 5 faces?

f) Which shape has 5 faces and 8 edges?

g) Which shape has the smallest number of faces? Does it also have the smallest number of edges? The smallest number of vertices?

BONUS ▶ Look at the number of vertices in prisms. Can a prism have an odd number of vertices? Explain.

G3-23 Shapes with Curved Surfaces

cones	cylinders	spheres

I. Circle the cones. Draw an ✗ on the cylinders. Write an S on the sphere.

A cone has one flat face, the base. The base is a circle.
A cone also has a **curved surface**.

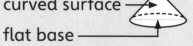

2. Shade the curved surface.

a)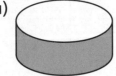

b)

c)

d)

e)

BONUS ▶

3. a) How many curved surfaces does a cylinder have? _____

b) How many curved surfaces does a sphere have? _____

c) How many bases does a cylinder have? _____

4. Match the shape to the name.

A.   B.   C.   D.   E.   F.

a) cylinder _____   b) square pyramid _____   c) rectangular prism _____

d) cone _____   e) triangular prism _____   f) triangular pyramid _____

5. a) Compare a cube and a square pyramid.

			Same?
Number of Faces			
Number of Triangular Faces			
Number of Square Faces			
Number of Edges			
Number of Vertices			

b) Compare a cone and a cylinder.

			Same?
Number of Flat Faces			
Number of Curved Surfaces			
Shape of Flat Faces			

6. Compare the shapes. Remember to include the number of faces, edges, and vertices, and the shapes of the faces.

a) 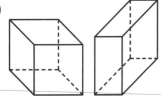　　b) 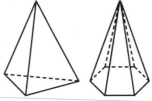　　c)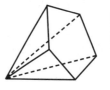

7. What shape am I?

a) I have 1 curved surface and no flat faces.

b) I have 5 faces. Only 1 of them is a rectangle.

BONUS ▶ I have 12 edges. They are all the same length. I am not a pyramid.

BONUS ▶ Six of my faces are squares. I am not a cube.

PDM3-4 Introduction to Pictographs

A pictograph uses symbols to show data.

On this pictograph, the symbol � means I student.

2 students eat lunch at home.

5 students eat lunch at school.

Lunch Location

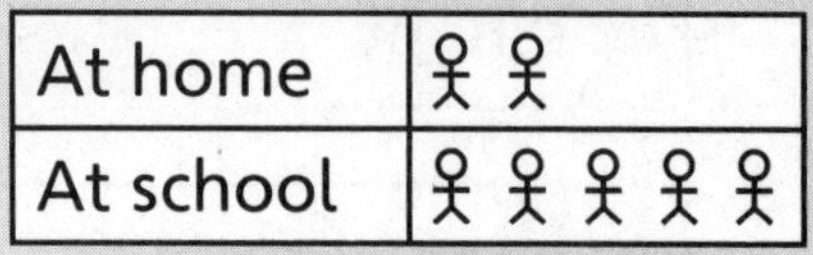

| At home | � � |
| At school | � � � � � |

1. Use the pictograph to answer the question.

Number of Rainy Days

April	◊ ◊ ◊ ◊ ◊ ◊ ◊ ◊
May	◊ ◊ ◊ ◊ ◊
June	◊ ◊ ◊ ◊
July	◊ ◊ ◊
August	◊ ◊ ◊ ◊
September	

◊ = I day

a) How many rainy days were there in each month?

June _____   May _____   August _____

b) Which month had only 3 rainy days? _____

c) Which months had the same number of rainy days? _____

d) How many more rainy days were there in April than in August? _____

e) June has 30 days. How many days were not rainy?

Write the subtraction equation. _____

f) September had 7 rainy days. Show this on the pictograph.

g) Which month had the most rainy days? _____

h) Which month had the fewest rainy days? _____

2. Use the pictograph to answer the questions.

a) **Lunch for Jay's Class** 🙂 = 1 student

At school	🙂 🙂 🙂 🙂 🙂 🙂 🙂
At home	🙂 🙂 🙂 🙂 🙂 🙂 🙂 🙂 🙂 🙂 🙂

Do more students from Jay's class eat lunch at home or

at school? _____ How many more? _____

b) **Lunch for Kate's Class** 🙂 = 1 student

At school	🙂 🙂　　🙂　　🙂 🙂　　🙂 🙂 🙂
At home	🙂 🙂 🙂 🙂 🙂　　🙂 🙂 🙂 🙂

Kate thinks more students eat lunch at school. Is she correct? _____

c) Fix the pictograph in part b) so that it is easier to read.

Lunch for Kate's Class 🙂 = 1 student

At school											
At home											

Do more students from Kate's class eat lunch at home or

at school? _____ How many more? _____

d) Use the data from the pictographs in parts a) and c) to make a new graph.

Lunch at School 🙂 = 1 student

Jay's class											
Kate's class											

Do more students from Jay's class or Kate's class

eat at school? _____ How many more? _____

3. Rob asked his friends to vote for their favourite sport.

a) Draw a circle for each student vote.

Favourite Sport	Number of Students
Baseball	5
Ice Hockey	6
Volleyball	3
Soccer	4

Students' Favourite Sports   ◯ = I student

Baseball	◯	◯	◯	◯	◯
Ice Hockey					
Volleyball					
Soccer					

b) Which sport is the most popular? _____

How can you see that from the pictograph? _____

_____

c) How many more students voted for baseball than for volleyball? _____

d) How many students in total voted for ball games? _____

BONUS ▶ How many more students voted for ball games than

for ice hockey? _____

4. Some students from Jane's class go to after-school programs.

a) Draw circles to show the data.

6 students go to art lessons.
3 more students go to soccer than to art lessons.
2 fewer students go to music lessons than to art lessons.

After-School Programs   ◯ = I student

Art									
Soccer									
Music									
No program									

b) There are 23 students in Jane's class. How many do not go to any after-school programs? Show this on the pictograph.

Probability and Data Management 3-4

PDM3-5 Pictographs

A **scale** shows what the symbol means on a pictograph.

10 students eat lunch at home and 20 students eat lunch at school. Both pictographs show the same data, but they use different scales.

Lunch Location

At home	�
At school	� �

Lunch Location

At home	� �
At school	� � � �

� = 10 students ←——— scale ———→ � = 5 students

1. Look at the scale and multiply to find what each group of symbols means.

   a) � = 5 people

   ��� = __15__ people   ����� = _____ people

   b) ✿ = 2 flowers

   ✿ ✿ = _____ flowers   ✿ ✿ ✿ ✿ = _____ flowers

   ✿ ✿ ✿ ✿ ✿ ✿ ✿ = _____ flowers

   c) ☐ = 3 boxes

   ☐☐☐ = _____ boxes   ☐☐☐☐☐ = _____ boxes

   ☐☐☐☐☐☐ = _____ boxes   ☐☐☐☐☐☐☐☐☐ = _____ boxes

BONUS ▶ If ☺ = 20 people, how many people is ☺ ☺ ☺ ☺ ☺ ? _____

2. Look at the scale and draw symbols to show each number.

   a) ☐ = 4 boxes

   12 boxes = ☐☐☐   8 boxes =

   b) ☐ = 5 boxes

   15 boxes =   30 boxes =

3. a) Use the pictograph to fill in the table.

Flowers in Evan's Garden   🌷 = 2 flowers

Roses	🌷 🌷 🌷 🌷
Pansies	🌷 🌷
Marigolds	🌷 🌷 🌷 🌷 🌷 🌷

Type of Flower	Number of Flowers
Roses	
Pansies	
Marigolds	

b) Use the data in part a) to draw a pictograph with the new scale.

Flowers in Evan's Garden   🌷 = 4 flowers

Roses					
Pansies					
Marigolds					

c) How many more marigolds than pansies does Evan have? _____

d) How many flowers does Evan have in total? _____

Half a symbol means half the number. Example: If 😊 = 4, then ◗ = 4 ÷ 2 = 2.

4. The first row shows what 😊 means. What does ◗ mean? Fill in the table.

😊	10	2	6	20	14	12	200
◗	5						

If 😊 = 10, then 😊 😊 😊 = 3 × 10 = 30, and 😊 😊 😊 ◗ = 30 + 5 = 35.

5. The first row shows what one symbol means. What does each group of symbols mean?

a)

☆	6	2	10
☆ ☆	12		
⧖	3		
☆ ☆ ⧖	15		

b)

🧍		2	4	10
🧍 🧍 🧍				
⧖				
🧍 🧍 🧍 🧍 ⧖				

Probability and Data Management 3-5

PDM3-6 Creating Pictographs

1. a) There are 25 shapes in the picture.
      Count the number of each shape.

Shape	Number of Shapes
Triangle	
Quadrilateral	
Pentagon	
Hexagon	
Circle	

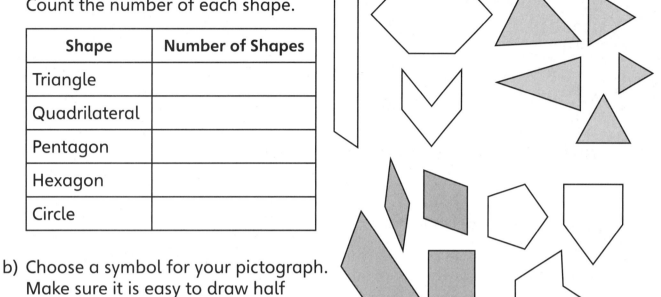

b) Choose a symbol for your pictograph.
   Make sure it is easy to draw half
   a symbol.

c) Draw a pictograph using your symbol.
   Remember to fill in the scale.

Shapes in the Picture

Triangle						
Quadrilateral						
Pentagon						
Hexagon						
Circle						

_____ = 2 shapes

d) What is the most common shape in the picture? _____

   What is the least common shape in the picture? _____

e) Polygons have straight sides.
   How many polygons are in the picture? _____

f) How many more polygons than circles are in the picture? _____

Probability and Data Management 3-6   187

2. The first line shows the data. Circle the best scale for the data.

a) 12, 6, 8

☆ = 2 ⬭(circled)

☆ = 5

☆ = 10

b) 30, 20, 40

☆ = 2

☆ = 3

☆ = 10

c) 9, 12, 6

☆ = 3

☆ = 5

☆ = 10

d) 25, 10, 35

☆ = 2

☆ = 3

☆ = 5

> **REMINDER ▸** The **mode** is the most common data value.
> In the set 3, 3, 4, 4, 4, 5, 5, 6, the mode is 4.

3. Lily counted the students in each grade at camp.

Draw a pictograph for the given scale.

Grade	1	2	3	4	5
Number of Students	15	10	20	5	10

a) ☺ = 5 students

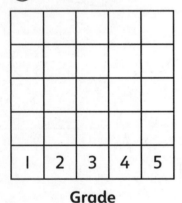

Grade

b) ☺ = 10 students

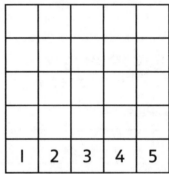

Grade

c) What is the mode? How can you find the mode from a pictograph?

4. Use the pictograph to answer the questions.

a) How many more students visited

Vancouver than Ottawa? _____

b) Fewer students visited Calgary than

Ottawa. How many fewer? _____

c) 15 more students visited Toronto than
Winnipeg. Show this on the pictograph.

Cities Visited by Students

Calgary, AB	◖
Toronto, ON	☺ ☺ ☺ ◖
Ottawa, ON	☺ ☺ ☺
Vancouver, BC	☺ ☺ ☺ ☺
Winnipeg, MB	

☺ = 10 students

Probability and Data Management 3-6

PDM3-7 Introduction to Bar Graphs

A **bar graph** uses **bars** to show data.

Each bar graph has a **title**, **labels**, two **axes**, and a **scale**.

This bar graph shows that there are 5 cats and 3 dogs in a shelter.

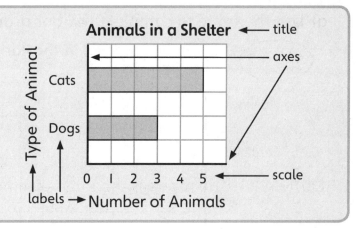

1. The bar graph shows fish at the zoo.

   a) Use the bar graph to fill in the table.

Type of Fish	Number of Fish
Bass	3
Catfish	
Perch	
Sunfish	

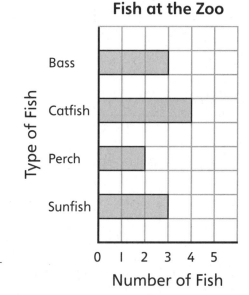

Fish at the Zoo

   b) What is the most common fish? _____

   c) What is the least common fish? _____

   d) How many fish are at the zoo in total? _____

2. Use the bar graph to answer the questions.

   a) How many students have black hair? _____

   b) How many students have blond hair? _____

   c) 2 students have red hair. Draw a bar for them.

   d) How many students do not have

      black hair? _____

   e) How many students are in the class? _____

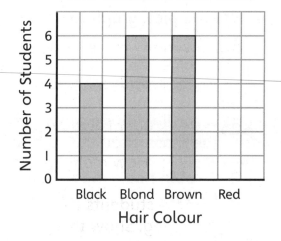

Hair Colours in Our Class

3. Arsham counted birds he saw in the park.

    a) Use the table to complete the bar graph.

Birds Seen in the Park

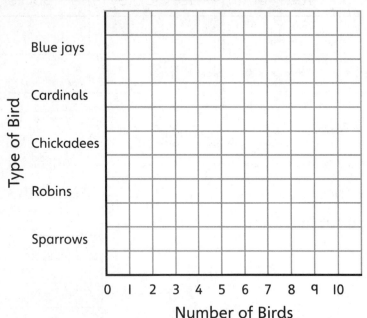

Type of Bird	Number of Birds
Blue jays	2
Cardinals	4
Chickadees	7
Robins	4
Sparrows	10

    b) What was the most common bird seen in the park? _____

       How does the bar graph show it? _____

    c) How many more sparrows than robins did Arsham see? _____

    d) How many birds did Arsham see in total? _____

    e) A blue jay has a mass of about 85 g. How much did the blue jays

       that Arsham saw weigh altogether? _____

    f) A sparrow has a mass of about 20 g. What weighs more,
       all the sparrows that Arsham saw or all the blue jays he saw?

    g) A chickadee has a mass of about 10 g. Do all the chickadees
       Arsham saw weigh more altogether than one blue jay?

    h) A cardinal has a mass of about 45 g. Use doubling to find
       the mass of all the cardinals Arsham saw.

    i) A robin has a mass of about 80 g. How much do all the robins
       that Arsham saw weigh altogether?

    BONUS ▶ What was the total mass of all the birds Arsham saw?

                                  Probability and Data Management 3-7

4. Amy asked her friends about their favourite sports and recorded the results in a tally chart.

Favourite Sport	Baseball	Volleyball	Ice Hockey	Soccer
Tally |卌 ||	||||	卌 ||||	||
Count				

a) Complete the "count" on Amy's tally chart.

b) Use Amy's tally chart to complete the bar graph below.

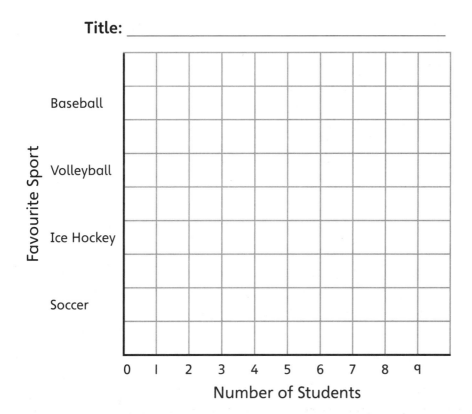

Title: _____

c) Which sport has the most data values? _____

How can you find that from the graph? _____

_____

d) Write two conclusions Amy can make from her data.

_____

_____

PDM3-8 Bar Graphs

Some bar graphs use skip counting in a scale.

1. Tessa asked her friends which juice they like best. She made a bar graph to show the results.

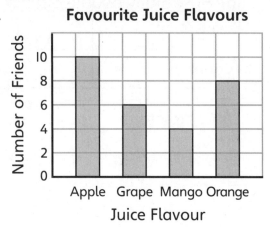

Favourite Juice Flavours

   a) What was the most popular flavour?

   _____

   b) What was the least popular flavour?

   _____

   c) Roy wants to bring the 2 most popular flavours of juice to a party. Which flavours of juice should he bring?

   _____

   d) What number does the scale skip count by? _____

   e) Skip count to fill in the table using the bar graph.

Juice Flavour	Apple	Grape	Mango	Orange
Number of Friends	10			

2. Rick asked his classmates if they liked travelling by car, plane, or train the most. He shows the answers in a bar graph.

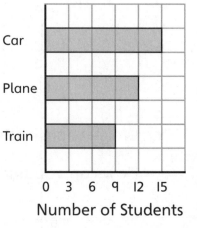

Favourite Ways to Travel

   a) What number does the scale skip count by? _____

   b) The bar for car travel is _____ blocks long.

   Each block shows _____ students.

   c) Use the bar graph to fill in the table.

Way to Travel	Number of Blocks	Multiplication	Number of Students
Car	5	5 × 3 = 15	15
Plane			
Train			

3. A national park asked 100 people to vote for their favourite activity in the park. Some results are shown in the table.

a) How many people did not choose cycling?

_____

b) How many people chose cycling? Write this number in the table.

c) What number does the scale in the bar graph

in part e) below count by? _____

Activity	Number of People
Boating	10
Cycling	
Hiking	15
Swimming	50

d) Fill in the table.

Activity	Number of People	Division	Length of Bar (Blocks)
Boating	10	10 ÷ 5 = 2	2
Cycling			
Hiking			
Swimming			

e) Finish the bar graph.

Favourite Activity in the Park

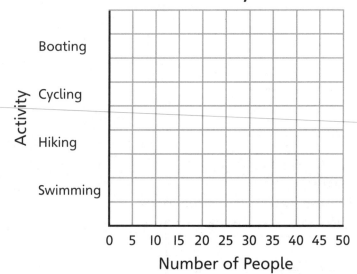

4. Grade 3 students collected coats for charity.

They collected 3 times as many coats in January as in December.

They collected 6 more coats in February than in December.

Altogether, they collected 18 coats.

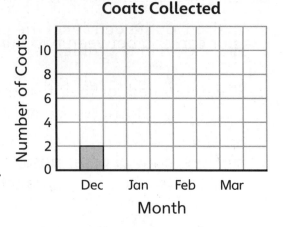

Coats Collected

a) Use the clues above to fill in the missing bars.

b) In which month did students collect the

most coats? _____

c) In which two months did students collect the same

number of coats? _____ and _____

d) How many fewer coats did students collect in March

than in February? _____

5. The bar graph shows how much snow fell in Ottawa, ON, during the year.

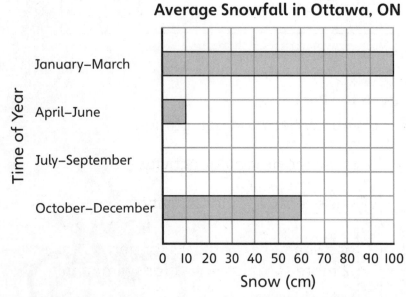

a) How many more centimetres of snow fell in the first three months of the year than in the last three months of the year?

b) How much snow fell in the whole year?

c) Which months have no bar? Explain why this makes sense.

Probability and Data Management 3-8

PDM3-9 Scales on Bar Graphs

> A bar can end between two numbers on a bar graph.

1. Students voted for their favourite summer activity. The bar graph shows the results.

    a) Fill in the table.

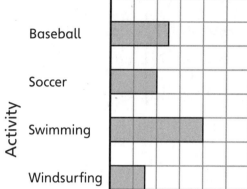

Favourite Summer Activity

Favourite Activity	Number of Students
Baseball	5
Soccer	
Swimming	
Windsurfing	

   b) 7 students picked boating. Add the bar for them to the bar graph.

   c) Fill in the blanks.

   _____ fewer students picked soccer than swimming.

   _____ more students picked swimming than baseball.

   _____ students picked water activities.

   _____ more students chose water activities than ball games.

   _____ was the most popular activity.

   _____ was the least popular activity.

BONUS ▶ Kevin thinks that the bar for swimming is 2 blocks longer than the bar for soccer, so 2 more students voted for swimming. Is he correct? Explain.

   _____

   _____

   _____

2. Jake and Hanna asked their classmates about pets. The bar graphs show the results.

Jake's bar graph:

Pets of Grade 3 Students

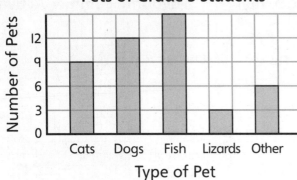

Hanna's bar graph:

Pets of Grade 3 Students

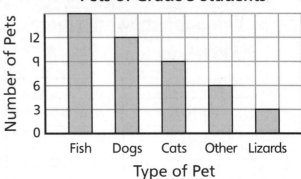

a) Fill in the table.

Type of Pet	Number of Pets	
	Jake's Graph	**Hanna's Graph**
Cats		
Dogs		
Fish		
Lizards		
Other		

b) Do the graphs show the same information? _____

Do the graphs look the same? _____

c) How did Jake choose to order the labels on the horizontal axis?

_____

How did Hanna choose to order the labels on the horizontal axis?

_____

d) Which pet was the most common? _____

On which graph is it easier to see that? _____

Probability and Data Management 3-9

3. Sara is researching different dog breeds.

a) Fill in the table using Bar Graph 1.

Dog Breed	Mass (kg)
Beagle (B)	
Collie (C)	
Dalmatian (D)	
Husky (H)	
Pug (P)	

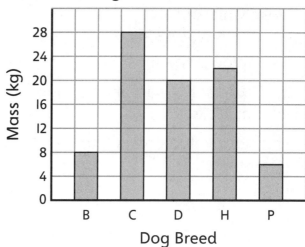

Bar Graph 1
Dog Breeds and Masses

b) What number does the scale

skip count by? _____

c) Are there bars that end between the numbers? _____

d) How many blocks long is the tallest bar? _____

e) Use the table to finish Bar Graph 2 with a scale that skip counts by 2 to show the same information.

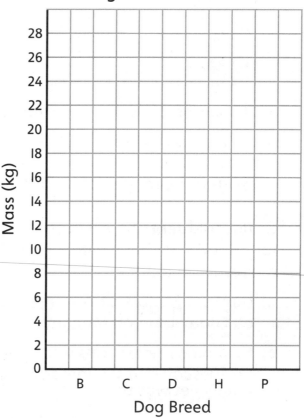

Bar Graph 2
Dog Breeds and Masses

f) Are there bars that end between

the numbers? _____

g) Which graph takes more space? _____

h) Use the graphs to say which dog breed has a mass 8 kg greater than a dalmatian.

_____

Which graph makes this easier

to answer? _____

i) Use the graphs to find out which breed weighs 22 kg less than a collie.

_____

Which graph makes this easier

to answer? _____

Some bar graphs are not drawn on a grid.

This bar graph shows that Vicky has 4 sports stickers, 8 animal stickers, and 5 food stickers.

The mode is the most common data value.

In Vicky's set of stickers the mode is animal stickers.

This data value occurs 8 times.

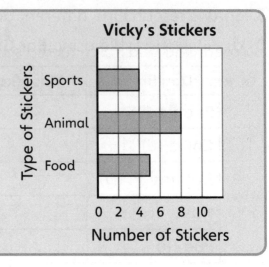

Vicky's Stickers

4. Students voted for their favourite breakfast.

   a) Fill in the table.

Type of Food	Number of Students
Cereal	
Eggs	
Pancakes	
Toast	
Waffles	

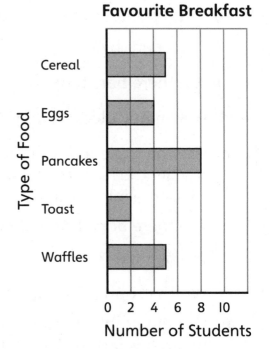

Favourite Breakfast

   b) How many more students voted for pancakes than for cereal? _____

   c) What is the mode on this bar graph? _____

5. Grade 3 students collected cans of food for a food bank for a week. They showed the results in a bar graph.

   a) How many more cans were collected on Friday than on Monday?

   b) How many fewer cans were collected on Tuesday and Wednesday together than on Friday?

   c) How many cans were collected in total?

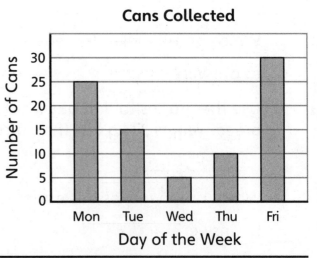

Cans Collected

Probability and Data Management 3-9

PDM3-10 Comparing Graphs

Karen, Sal, and Yu collected some leaves. They each made a graph.

Karen's graph:

Leaves Collected

Beech	◊	◊	◊	◊	
Elm	◊	◊	◊		
Willow	◊	◊	◊	◊	◊

Sal's graph:

Leaves Collected

Yu's graph:

Lengths of Leaves

1. a) What type of graph did each student draw?

   Karen: _____ Sal: _____ Yu: _____

   b) What does each graph have? Write ✓ or ✗.

Feature	Pictograph	Bar Graph	Line Plot
Title			
Labels			
Number line			
Vertical axis			
Scale			
Symbols			

   c) How many leaves did Karen, Sal, and Yu collect? _____
   How does each graph show this?

   Pictograph: _____

   Bar graph: _____

   Line plot: _____

2. Use the graphs that Karen, Sal, and Yu made to answer the question. Say which graph or graphs you could use to answer the question.

		Answer	Graph(s)
a)	How many more willow leaves than beech leaves did they collect?	1	*pictograph, bar graph*
b)	How many fewer elm leaves than beech leaves did they collect?		
c)	How many leaves longer than 12 cm did they collect?		
d)	How many fewer 14 cm long leaves than 10 cm long leaves were there?		
e)	What was the most common type of leaf?		

3. Students voted for their favourite type of book.

a) Make a bar graph showing the same data as the pictograph.

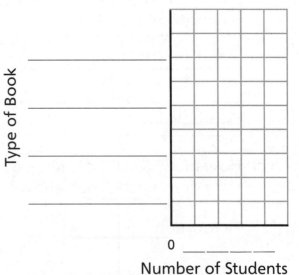

Favourite Type of Book

| Fantasy | Sci-fi | Short stories | Non-fiction |

= 1 student

b) How many more students voted for fantasy books than for science fiction?

c) How many fewer students voted for non-fiction books than for short stories?

I. Megan asked her classmates to circle their favourite season.
   She gave them the choices below.

   Spring   Summer   Winter

   a) Are there enough choices? _____ Explain. _____

   _____

   b) What choice should she add? _____

2. Alex asked his classmates to circle the number of siblings
   (brothers or sisters) they have. He offered the answers below.

   0   I   2   3

   Anne has 4 siblings, and Carl has 6 siblings.

   a) Can Anne and Carl answer the survey? _____

   b) What **one** choice could Alex add so that both Carl and Anne

      can answer the survey? _____

3. Ask your classmates how they got to school today.

   a) Tally your results.

   Title: _____

Way to Get to School	Tally
School bus	
Car	
Walk	
Bike	
Scooter	
Other	

   b) Make a pictograph. = 2 students

To write a survey question,

- Decide what you want to know.

    Example:
    What is the favourite fruit of my classmates?

- Make sure the question does not have too many possible responses. One of the responses could be "other."

    Example:
    What is your favourite fruit?   ✗ This question may give you too many answers.

    What fruit do you like?   ✗ People could give more than one answer.
    ☐ apple ☐ grape ☐ orange ☐ other

    Which is your favourite fruit?   ✓ This is a better survey question.
    ☐ apple ☐ grape ☐ orange ☐ other

4. a) Write a survey question to find out what pizza toppings students like best.

    _____

    _____

    _____

   b) Write the possible responses to your question.

    ☐ _____   ☐ _____   ☐ _____

    ☐ _____   ☐ _____   ☐ other

5. Write a different survey question you could ask your classmates.

    _____

    _____

    _____

Probability and Data Management 3-11

6. a) Survey your classmates to find out their favourite school subjects.
Use the table to tally and count your results.

School Subject	Tally	Count
English		
French		
Gym		
Math		
Science		
Other		

b) What scale (counting by 1s, 2s, 3s, 5s, or 10s) would be the best

for a bar graph of your data? _____ Explain. _____

_____

c) Use the scale you picked in part b). Create a bar graph
of the data you collected.

Title: _____

School Subject

English

French

Gym

Math

Science

Other

0 __ __ __ __ __ __ __ __ __ __

Number of Students

d) List three conclusions you can make from your bar graph.

PDM3-12 Outcomes

When you roll a die, spin a spinner, or play a game, the results are called **outcomes**.

Alice plays a game of cards with a friend. There are three possible outcomes:

1. Alice wins.
2. Alice loses.
3. There is a **tie** or **draw**. The game ends and nobody wins or loses.

1. List all the possible outcomes of spinning the spinner. How many outcomes are there in total?

a)

spin 5, spin 6

_____

Number of outcomes: __2__

b)

_____

_____

Number of outcomes: _____

c)

_____

_____

Number of outcomes: _____

d)

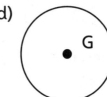

_____

_____

Number of outcomes: _____

2. Fill in the table.

		Possible Outcomes	Number of Outcomes
a)	tossing a coin	_heads, tails_	2
b)	rolling a regular die		
c)	playing soccer		

3. You take a ball out of the box. How many outcomes are there?

a)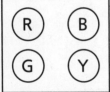

b)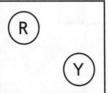

c)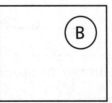

d)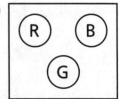

_____ outcomes   _____ outcomes   _____ outcomes   _____ outcomes

Spinning the spinner has four outcomes:

   1. The pointer lands in the blue region at top right.
   2. The pointer lands in the blue region at bottom right.
   3. The pointer lands in the blue region at bottom left.
   4. The pointer lands in the red region.

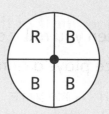

4. How many outcomes are there in total when you spin the spinner
    or take a ball from the box?

a)

_____ outcomes

b)

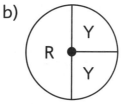

_____ outcomes

c)

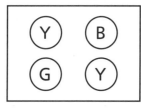

_____ outcomes

d)

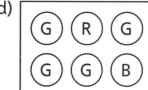

_____ outcomes

5. a) How many outcomes are there when taking a marble

     out of the box without looking? _____

  b) How many outcomes are there of taking out

     a red marble? _____

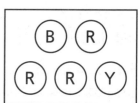

6. How many outcomes does the spinner have? How many outcomes
    are there of spinning white?

a)

    Number of outcomes: _____

    Number of white outcomes: _____

b)

    Number of outcomes: _____

    Number of white outcomes: _____

PDM3-13 Even Chance

1. Shade **half** of the pieces.

a)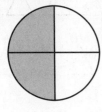

_2_ pieces in half a pie

_4_ pieces in a pie

b)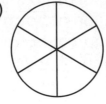

____ pieces in half a pie

____ pieces in a pie

c)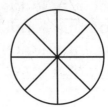

____ pieces in half a pie

____ pieces in a pie

d)

____ pieces in half a pie

____ pieces in a pie

e)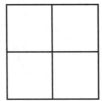

____ pieces in half a box

____ pieces in a box

f)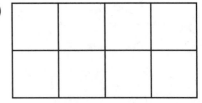

____ pieces in half a box

____ pieces in a box

2. Divide by 2.

a) $8 \div 2 =$ _____   b) $4 \div 2 =$ _____   c) $6 \div 2 =$ _____   d) $10 \div 2 =$ _____

e) $20 \div 2 =$ _____   f) $18 \div 2 =$ _____   g) $2 \div 2 =$ _____   h) $14 \div 2 =$ _____

3. Fill in the table.

Number	10	8	14	16
Half the Number	5			
Sum	_5_ + _5_ = 10	___ + ___ = 8	___ + ___ = 14	___ + ___ = 16

4. Circle half the lines to divide into two equal sets.

a)

b) | | | | | | | |

c) | | | | | | | | | | | | | |

d)

Probability and Data Management 3-13

5. Circle half the triangles.

a)

b)

c)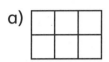

6. Shade 1 less than half of the squares.

a)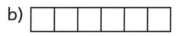

b)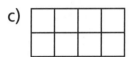

c)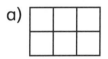

d)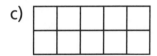

7. Shade one more than half of the squares.

a)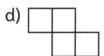

b)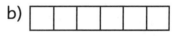

c)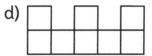

d)

8. Is the first number more than half, half, or less than half of the second number? Hint: Find half of the second number first.

a) 2 is ___*less than half*___ of 6.

b) 3 is _____ of 8.

c) 5 is _____ of 12.

d) 6 is _____ of 10.

e) 9 is _____ of 18.

f) 5 is _____ of 16.

g) 9 is _____ of 12.

h) 10 is _____ of 14.

i) 6 is _____ of 8.

j) 7 is _____ of 10.

k) 3 is _____ of 6.

l) 4 is _____ of 6.

9. How many parts of the spinner are shaded? How many parts are there in total? Circle the spinner if exactly half the spinner is shaded.

a)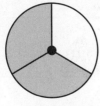

b)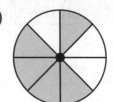

c)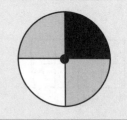

_____ parts shaded

_____ parts shaded

_____ parts shaded

_____ parts in total

_____ parts in total

_____ parts in total

Half of the spinner is grey. You expect to spin grey half the time.

There is an **even chance** of spinning grey.

10. Count the shaded and unshaded regions. Circle the spinners that have an even chance of spinning grey.

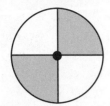 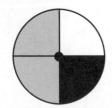 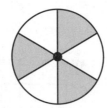  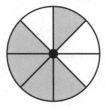 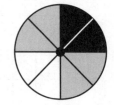

11. Six marbles are in a box. Three of them are yellow.

a) Are exactly half the marbles yellow? _____

b) Is there an even chance of taking out a yellow marble? _____

12. Twelve marbles are in a box. Seven of them are green.

a) Are exactly half the marbles green? _____

b) Is there an even chance of taking a green marble? _____

13. A hockey team plays 12 games and wins 7 of them. Does the team win more than half the games? Explain.

BONUS ▶ A basketball team won 4 out of their last 6 games. Based on the last 6 games, does the team have an even chance to win? Explain.

Probability and Data Management 3-13

PDM3-14 Even, Likely, and Unlikely

1. How often do you expect to spin white? Write "more than half the time," "half the time," or "less than half the time."

a)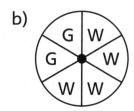

b)

c)

_____   _____   _____

_____   _____   _____

d)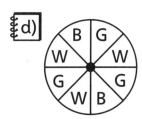

e)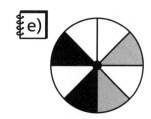

f)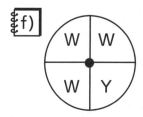

> When you describe the result of a game, rolling a die, or spinning a spinner, you describe an **event**.
>
> You expect an **even** event to happen exactly half the time.
>
> You expect a **likely** event to happen more than half the time.
>
> You expect an **unlikely** event to happen less than half the time.

2. Describe the event as "likely" or "unlikely."

a)

b)

c)

Spinning green is   Spinning red is   Spinning yellow is

_____ .   _____ .   _____ .

3. Describe the chances of the event as "unlikely," "even," or "likely."

a) 8 marbles in a box, 4 red marbles
   Event: You take out a red marble.

b) 10 marbles in a box, 6 red marbles
   Event: You take out a red marble.

c) 6 socks in a drawer, 4 black socks
   Event: You pull out a black sock.

d) 12 coins in a pocket, 3 dimes
   Event: You take out a dime.

If an event cannot happen, it is **impossible**. Rolling the number 8 on a die is impossible because a die only has the numbers 1, 2, 3, 4, 5, and 6 on its faces.

If an event must happen, it is **certain**. When you roll a die, it is certain that you will roll a number less than 7.

You will **likely** spin yellow on the spinner in the picture. You are **unlikely** to spin red.

4. Write "certain," "likely," "unlikely," or "impossible" to describe the chances of the event.

a)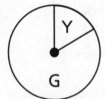

Spinning green is

_____ .

b)

Spinning yellow is

_____ .

c)

Spinning red is

_____ .

d)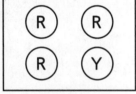

Picking red is

_____ .

e)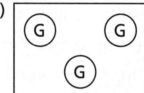

Picking green is

_____ .

f)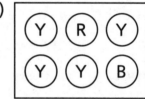

Picking yellow is

_____ .

g)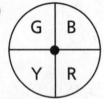

Spinning yellow is

_____ .

h)

Spinning green is

_____ .

i)

Spinning red is

_____ .

5. Which colour of marble are you more likely to take, red or blue? Explain your thinking.

Probability and Data Management 3-14

PDM3-15 Fair Games

1. How many outcomes are there? Are all the outcomes equal?

a)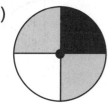

b)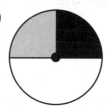

c)

d)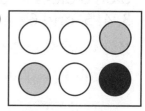

___4___ outcomes   ___3___ outcomes   _____ outcomes   _____ outcomes

___Equal___   ___Not equal___   _____   _____

A game is **fair** if all players have the same chances to win. You can check if a game is fair:

Step 1: Check that all outcomes are equal.

Step 2: Count how many outcomes give each player a win.

If the number of winning outcomes is the same for all players, the game is fair.

---

2. How many winning outcomes does each player have?

a) Player 1 wins if he spins white. Player 2 wins if she spins grey.

   Player 1 has ___2___ winning outcomes.

   Player 2 has ___4___ winning outcomes.

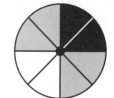

b) Player 1 wins if he tosses heads. Player 2 wins if he tosses tails.

   Player 1 has _____ winning outcome.

   Player 2 has _____ winning outcome.

c) Player 1 wins if she rolls 1. Player 2 wins if he rolls 2. Player 3 wins if she rolls 3, 4, or 6.

   Player 1 has _____ winning outcome.

   Player 2 has _____ winning outcome.

   Player 3 has _____ winning outcomes.

3. In which part in Question 2 is the game fair? _____

4. Write "true" or "not true".

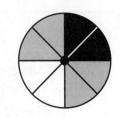

a) Players spin the spinner shown. Player 1 wins by spinning black.
Player 2 wins by spinning grey.

The outcomes are equal. _True_

All players have the same number of winning outcomes. _Not true_

The game is fair. _Not true_

b) Players roll a regular die. Player 1 wins by rolling a 1.
Player 2 wins by rolling a 6.

The outcomes are equal. _____

All players have the same number of winning outcomes. _____

The game is fair. _____

c) Players roll a regular die. Player 1 wins by rolling a 1 or a 2.
Player 2 wins by rolling a 5 or a 6.

The outcomes are equal. _____

All players have the same number of winning outcomes. _____

The game is fair. _____

d) Players pull a marble out of the box shown without
looking. Player 1 wins if he picks a grey marble. Player 2
wins if she picks a black marble.

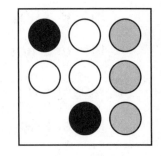

The outcomes are equal. _____

All players have the same number of winning outcomes.

_____

The game is fair. _____

e) Players pull a marble out of the box shown without
looking. Player 1 wins if he picks a grey marble. Player 2
wins if she picks a black marble. Player 3 wins if he picks
a white marble.

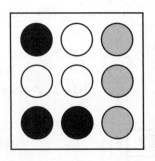

The outcomes are equal. _____

All players have the same number of winning outcomes.

_____

The game is fair. _____

Probability and Data Management 3-15

5. Who has a better chance of winning? If the chances are the same, write "The game is fair."

a) Players pick marbles from a box without looking. If the marble is grey, Player 1 wins. If the marble is white, Player 2 wins.

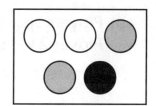

_____

b) Players throw darts at the board in the picture. If the dart hits black, Player 1 wins. If the dart hits white, Player 2 wins.

_____

c) Players spin the spinner in the picture. If they spin grey, Player 1 wins. If they spin black, Player 2 wins. If they spin white, Player 3 wins.

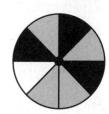

_____

d) Players take marbles from a box without looking. If the marble is black, Player 1 wins. If the marble is white, Player 2 wins. If the marble is striped, Player 3 wins.

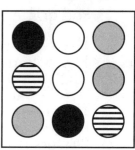

_____

6. Anton wants to spin blue to win. Emma wants to spin yellow to win. Draw a spinner with at least 4 regions and colour according to the given chances.

a) Anton has more chances to win.

b) Emma has more chances to win.

c) The game is fair.

BONUS ▶ Draw a spinner with at least 6 regions so that Emma has more chances to win.

7. Players pick one of the 5 cards in the picture without looking. If the number is less than 4, Player 1 wins. If the number is 4 or more, Player 2 wins. Is the game fair? Explain.

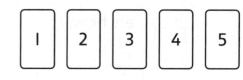

PDM3-16 Expectation

Half the spinner is red. We expect to spin red half the time.

One quarter of the spinner is blue. We expect to spin blue a quarter of the time.

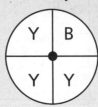

1. David wins with a red spin. Jax wins with a green spin. They spin the spinner 20 times.

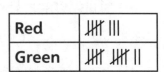

   a) How many times would you expect each player to win?

   David: _____ times   Jax: _____ times

   b) The tally shows the result of the game. Jax says

   the game was not fair. Do you agree? _____

Red	卌 lll
Green	卌 卌 ll

2. a) Flip a coin 30 times and make a tally of the number of heads and tails.

Outcome	Tally	Count
Heads		
Tails		

   b) If you flip a coin repeatedly, what fraction of the time would you expect

   to flip heads? Half? More than half? Less than half? _____

3. a) If you roll a die 20 times, how many times do you expect

   to roll an even number (2, 4, or 6)? _____

   b) How many times do you expect to roll an odd number (1, 3, or 5)? _____

   c) Roll a die 20 times. Make a tally of your results.

Outcome	Tally	Count
Even number (2, 4, or 6)		
Odd number (1, 3, or 5)		

   Did your results match your expectations? _____

4. Use a paper clip. Hold a pencil and spin the paper clip around the tip of the pencil.

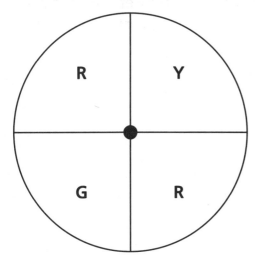 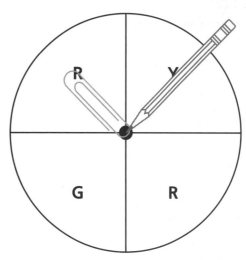

a) If you spin the spinner 20 times, how many times would you predict spinning red? _____

b) Spin the spinner 20 times. Make a tally of your results.

Did your results match your expectations? _____

Colour	Tally	Count
Red		
Green		
Yellow		

5. You play a board game with the spinner below.

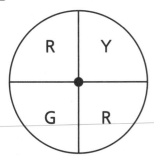

Colour	Move
Red	forwards I space
Green	backwards I space
Yellow	miss a turn

a) Using the spinner, are you likely to miss a turn? Explain.

b) Using the spinner, which way are you more likely to move, forwards or backwards?

c) Design a spinner in which you are more likely to move backwards.